D0010964

THE PHONE BOOK

The Curious History
of the Book That Everyone
Uses But No One Reads

☎

Ammon Shea

A PERIGEE BOOK

A PERIGEE BOOK
Published by the Penguin Group
Penguin Group (USA) Inc.
375 Hudson Street, New York, New York 10014, USA

Penguin Group (Canada), 90 Eglinton Avenue East, Suite 700, Toronto, Ontario M4P 2Y3, Canada
(a division of Pearson Penguin Canada Inc.)
Penguin Books Ltd., 80 Strand, London WC2R 0RL, England
Penguin Group Ireland, 25 St. Stephen's Green, Dublin 2, Ireland (a division of Penguin Books Ltd.)
Penguin Group (Australia), 250 Camberwell Road, Camberwell, Victoria 3124, Australia
(a division of Pearson Australia Group Pty. Ltd.)
Penguin Books India Pvt. Ltd., 11 Community Centre, Panchsheel Park, New Delhi—110 017, India
Penguin Group (NZ), 67 Apollo Drive, Rosedale, North Shore 0632, New Zealand
(a division of Pearson New Zealand Ltd.)
Penguin Books (South Africa) (Pty.) Ltd., 24 Sturdee Avenue, Rosebank, Johannesburg 2196,
South Africa
Penguin Books Ltd., Registered Offices: 80 Strand, London WC2R 0RL, England

While the author has made every effort to provide accurate telephone numbers and Internet addresses at the time of publication, neither the publisher nor the author assumes any responsibility for errors, or for changes that occur after publication. Further, the publisher does not have any control over and does not assume any responsibility for author or third-party websites or their content.

First edition: October 2010

Library of Congress Cataloging-in-Publication Data

Shea, Ammon.
    The phone book : the curious history of the book that everyone uses but no one reads / Ammon Shea.—1st ed.
        p. cm.
    Includes bibliographical references and index.
    ISBN 978-0-399-53593-2
    1. Telephone—Directories—History. I. Title.
    HE8721.S54 2010
    364.6025—dc22   2010022308

PRINTED IN THE UNITED STATES OF AMERICA

10   9   8   7   6   5   4   3   2   1

Most Perigee books are available at special quantity discounts for bulk purchases for sales promotions, premiums, fund-raising, or educational use. Special books, or book excerpts, can also be created to fit specific needs. For details, write: Special Markets, Penguin Group (USA) Inc., 375 Hudson Street, New York, New York 10014.

For Ogden

The new phone book's here! The new phone book's here!

The end product is a garden-variety white pages directory, devoid of even the slightest trace of creativity.

ACKNOWLEDGMENTS

My thanks are due, as always, to Jim Rutman, for continuing to be the sort of agent that writers always hope to have as representation. And similarly, thanks are due to Marian Lizzi and Christina Lundy of Perigee, who tirelessly (and patiently) worked to make this book far better than the one that I initially wrote.

Charles Eric Gordon, Gwillim Law, and Madeline Schwartzman were all kind enough to spend time telling me their telephone book stories, enchanting me in the process. And David Smith, who has recently retired from his position as "the most helpful librarian that the New York Public Library has ever had," provided great assistance in too many ways to count.

And my thanks to and for Alix, who can make any writing, and any anything, better than one has any right to hope for.

CONTENTS

INTRODUCTION

A wonderful and picturesque story about telephone books appears in an old railroad journal from 1935. An unnamed fruit company in Central America was having difficulty with local bandits, who were hijacking its trains. The train cars were built of steel, and while this may have once rendered them impervious to most forms of attack, the bandits in question had adopted the use of high-powered bullets, which proved more than capable of penetrating the sides of the cars. Obviously, a better form of protection was needed.

There is no mention of how the happy discovery was made, but someone found that the Manhattan telephone book was the exact same thickness as the partitions inside the steel walls of the train cars and would stay there when slipped in. Filled to the brim with telephone books, the trains would be effectively bulletproof. So the fruit company ordered four thousand pounds of old telephone books from Manhattan and had them inserted into the train cars. I presume the bandits gnashed their teeth in fury at being so thwarted by outdated home reference books and resigned themselves to being impecunious footnotes in this fine tale.

The problem with this story is that it repeats itself in a variety of decades, in a variety of forms. A 1963 story in the *Chicago Tribune* says that it was "the president of a volatile Latin American republic" who ordered the telephone books for his private railroad car.[1] The *New York Times* gives some conflicting accounts: in a story from 1946 it states that the directories were intended to guard trains by stopping the bullets from the rifles of "revolutionists,"[2] but three years later another article claims that the telephone books were bought by the Chiriqui Land Company, to guard the pay trucks from bandits.[3]

And a poem by William Price Turner, written in the 1960s, begins with the line "Eight hundred telephone directories will bulletproof a truck, claims a fruit company in South America," before going on to describe a bandit attack on a truck. The poem unfortunately gives no documentation that might yield any authenticity to this tale, but that is the nature of poetry. And it does include the (I hope) immortal line "The desert bristles with rifles and vexed mustaches," so I am more than willing to forgive the lack of footnotes.

Variations of this story have also appeared in the *New Yorker*, a number of railroad magazines, and newspapers both great and not so great. Sometimes the doughty telephone books are defending against bandits (or revolutionists) in Central America, and other times they are guarding the funds or persons of some entity in South America.

None of the articles offers a follow-up, so there is no information as to whether the fruit company was no longer plagued by its bandits, or whether the president of the unnamed country lived to a ripe old age, endlessly and blissfully rolling along the rails in his private car, protected by millions and millions of telephone numbers. Perhaps the bandits, rather than resigning themselves to so ignominious a fate as being thwarted by cheap paper and even cheaper ink, got themselves and their vexed mustaches a bazooka or a howitzer and soon after blew up the entire vehicle.

It is hard to say whether this tale is a colorful bit of invented history or the telephone books actually proved to be such a useful and well-known ballistic prophylactic that they were used for this purpose in a variety of times and places.

But even if it is apocryphal to the point of almost certainly being fiction, the tale is still illustrative of our relationship with the telephone book. There is perhaps no other book that has been so useful and yet so often regarded as useless.

In addition to possibly serving as protection from bullets, telephone books have served as impressive-looking books for strongmen (and the occasional strongwoman) to rip in half. They have been a stage prop for the brilliant (and very short—five feet, two inches) jazz pianist Errol Garner and used as dinner table risers for uncountable millions of children over the past hundred years. They have been turned into everything from handbags to ceiling tiles to more telephone books.

During World War II, the Wright Aeronautical Corporation used telephone books in the construction of Whirlwind and Cyclone aircraft engines, as a means of keeping dirt out of the castings when they were poured (the thin, cheap paper burned away easily and didn't leave any residue). They have been put to such exultant uses as confetti for ticker-tape parades and to such inglorious ones as kitty litter.

They are the only books I know of that have come with instructions printed inside calling for their own destruction, a sort of "burn after reading" notice and an attempt by the telephone company to prevent the retention of outdated information.

While it may indeed be deserving of the bookish oblivion toward which it so surely seems to be headed, is the telephone book truly not worth our attention at all? Is it not odd that the book that has been printed more than any other book in the history of the printed word (hundreds of times more, in fact) and that has been a part of the lives of so many should remain so unexamined?

There has never been a book written about the telephone book. One might excuse this oversight, since for most of its brief history, whenever it is mentioned, the telephone book is held up as an example of either "something large" or "the most boring thing ever printed." On some occasions it is reputed to have served both purposes, such as when senators putatively read the telephone book out loud in an attempt to filibuster legislation.

Not only have no books been written about this most useful and quotidian of tomes, but there has also never been a dissertation written about it. This is somewhat more surprising when one considers that PhD dissertations are typically more concerned with examining some previously unexamined topic than they are with providing reader excitement. Looking over the field just in the last decade, one can find PhD candidates who have successfully achieved their degrees with such topics as "Ultimate spin: Contesting the rhetoric, countercultural ethos and commodification of the Ultimate 'Frisbee' sport, 1968–2008" and "The effect of spirituality during golf performance" (which was done at Northern Illinois University in 2008 and should not be confused with the 2007 dissertation presented at the University of Nevada, "Inner experience during golf performance").

A very small number of academic papers have given credit to the telephone book, but most of them are not about the book itself; and insofar as they mention the telephone book, it is simply as a tool that allows the collecting of information for a sociological survey.

Is the telephone book indeed so unworthy of consideration? I am not interested in making the claim, as has become popular of late with nonfiction books about a small subject, that this is somehow "the book that changed the world." Judging by the recent literature of adoxography (a sorely underused word that means "good writing on a trivial subject"), there have been many overlooked things that have changed the world.

In the last ten years alone, books with the phrase "changed the world" in their titles have been published on the 1960 Olympics, a map, a speck, the banana, the color mauve, tea, codfish, the Atlantic Ocean, the Kalashnikov rifle, the Beatles' 1964 tour, the cable (wire), and the year AD 33 (and the years 1968 and 1917). If you enter this portentous phrase in WorldCat—the database of works held in libraries worldwide—you will see that the following things have also (according to book titles) "changed the world": ten choices, twenty-four hours, fifteen battles, five machines, twelve months, twenty-five inventions, fifty military leaders, twenty pieces of music, fifty shoes, one hundred maps, twenty-eight great ideas, five equations, eight hundred and sixty-five days, one hundred photographs, and ten books.

I am an enormous fan of these types of books, even though I am always slightly skeptical that their subject has changed the world significantly more than any number of other things. I am not interested in making the case that the telephone book has somehow, unbeknownst to us, toppled regimes in Central Europe or changed the world as we know it today by facilitating the spread of whooping cough through a nation.

I am interested in the role that it has played in our lives. Not so very long ago it would not have been a stretch to say that everyone has read at least some small portion of this book. When the phrase "I'm in the book" was spoken, it was immediately understood that the book in question referred to the telephone book. (This use appears to date from at least 1925, when a character in Agatha Christie's *Secrets of Chimneys* says, "You might ring up a number for me now. Look it up in the book.") With the deadly and inexorable march of progress, it appears less and less likely that this will continue to be true; in fact, I am certain that there are now many people below a certain age who have never experienced the gentle smudge of telephone book ink on their fingers.

Bleach Bottle Boutique, published in 1973, is more or less what one might fear it is—an arts and crafts book for what to do with all those pesky bleach bottles that end up lying about the house, unused and unloved once the bleach has been dispensed with. It is a small volume, this *Bleach Bottle Boutique*, some forty-three pages, but one can learn many things from it—how to create a megaphone from a used bleach bottle or the proper way to turn an empty container of Clorox into an ersatz pig that can then be proudly displayed on the lawn or the mantelpiece.*

Have we really become a people that is (to any extent) more willing to have a book about the uses of an empty bleach bottle than to have one that in any way explores the mysteries, such as they are, of the telephone book?

The big book may not be so very useful for disinfecting syringes or for whitening clothes, but that should not be taken as a sign that it is of no import in our lives. For most of the past century, it was the way that people found each other. Billions and billions of times it has provided small yet important bits of information—on an obvious level, where people lived and how to contact them, but it could also tell you how long they had lived there, who they lived with, and myriad other details that were not easily found in the age before the Internet. And this is to say nothing of all the secondary and tertiary ways in which the telephone book has been put to use.

Pause for a moment to consider all of the things that it is safe to assume have been accomplished many times over through the use of the telephone book. It has been used innumerable times to store something, as a sort of poor man's safe. Not a terribly effective safe, mind you, but it did perform this function nonetheless. It has been used for pressing leaves and saving old letters. It has

---

* And this is by no means the only book ever published about the uses of discarded bleach bottles; it is part of a much larger oeuvre that contains such varied works as *Christmas Decorations from Plastic Bottles*, *More Plastic Bottle Projects*, *Plastic Bottle Fun*, and *Toys to Make from Plastic Bottles*.

served a role in facilitating countless marriages, as for many years it assuredly provided the telephone number of the man or woman one wished to ask out on a date, which would eventually lead to romance and marriage (granted, once we reached the 1970s, this would in half the cases of marriage also lead to divorce, so let no one say that the telephone book is not a vengeful god).

An article in the journal of the Southern New England Telephone Company in 1936 made the case for the importance of the telephone book, in a tone that would indicate that it was already an oft-overlooked volume: "Names in the telephone book are more than names. They are friendships and homes and families. They are buyers and sellers of all that comes to market. They are bridge games and golf games. They are success in social life."[4]

It has given us billions of small frustrations when, in the hands of telemarketers, it became a means of interrupting dinner with unsolicited phone calls. It has been used to create a poorly sampled body of data, such as when the polls in the presidential race between Dewey and Truman all assured the prognosticators that Dewey would triumph (Dewey was certainly favored by people who owned telephones at the time).

For many decades telephone books were one of the first signifiers that a person had moved into a new home, a new neighborhood, a new state—they were a sign of change and, one can imagine, a portent of a new chapter in life.

If we are a society that has decided there is more value to be had in a book about what one can do with an (admittedly very clean) used plastic bottle than there is to be found in the history of a tome that has touched the lives of untold millions of people, then perhaps there is truly no hope for us.

But hope, much like the chemical composition of a bottle that once held bleach or some other cleaning fluid, is a tenacious thing. And it is my fond hope that now, in what would appear to be the twilight of the life of the telephone directory, we can finally have a look at this most humble, ephemeral, and useful of volumes—the telephone book.

1

THE FIRST PHONE BOOK

Considering that the telephone is a relatively recent invention and, furthermore, one that has inarguably changed the lives of all humans, there is a surprising lack of agreement as to who invented it.

We've all been taught that the telephone was developed by Alexander Graham Bell. It turns out that this may not be strictly true, although we're certainly much more familiar with his name than with the names of other claimants. Those who dig a little deeper than their elementary school textbooks are liable to find that Bell was no more the first person to create a telephone than Thomas Edison was the first person to create a telegraph.

Many people who are in a more informed position hold forth that one Elisha Gray was the inventor. Even though Gray himself is obviously long dead and past caring, these people will care on his behalf and will do so quite vociferously.

In one of the many curiously overlooked facets of American history, the inventor Elisha Gray appears to have been cheated out of his rightful position in the order of telephone inventors. In 1876, Gray, who went on to become one of the cofounders of Western Electric, filed a caveat, rather than a patent, for the invention, whereas Bell filed a full patent application.* Bell was helped considerably in his later efforts to make his telephone work when a patent office worker informed him of some of the contents of Elisha Gray's caveat.[1] Although many scholars of telephonic history disagree on which of the two men did in fact invent the first working telephone, it seems clear that Bell was helped considerably more by Gray's efforts than is acknowledged.

Let us not mourn Gray's fate too much. He fared much better than most other putative inventors: although denied the historic plaudits that Bell received, he ended up earning far more money from the telephone than Bell did. His earnings came from the more than seventy electrical patents he ended up holding, many of which dealt with telephony.[2]

The story doesn't end with Gray, even though he appears to have the strongest claim for the mantle of telephone inventor. Others claim that the true honor goes to Antonio Meucci, an Italian immigrant to the United States who was allegedly bamboozled out of his patent by unscrupulous means. Meucci had filed a caveat for his telephone in 1871, and continued to renew it yearly until 1875, at which point, it is said, he no longer had the

---

* Until the beginning of the twentieth century, people could file caveats with the U.S. Patent Office. A caveat was more or less an announcement that one intended to file a patent for a particular thing in the immediate future.

funds to do so. Meucci has supporters who have attempted to award him credit posthumously for inventing the telephone, and in 2002 the U.S. House of Representatives passed a resolution that honored him for his work and stated, "Whereas, if Meucci had been able to pay the $10 fee to maintain the caveat after 1874, no patent could have been issued to Bell." However, less than two weeks after this resolution passed, the government of Canada passed its own resolution, which asserted once again that Bell (who, although born in Scotland, spent much of his life in Nova Scotia) was in fact the true inventor of the telephone.

The story of the invention of the telephone may also be said to have begun some decade and a half earlier. Johann Phillip Reis, a German inventor, developed a telephone in 1861 that was capable of transmitting sounds but not of effectively reproducing speech. This not-so-minor impediment did not prevent numerous others from seizing upon Reis's invention as a means of filing lawsuits against Bell's patent, arguing that their designs were based on the Reis telephone and thus antedated the one created by Bell. Herbert Casson, in his book *The History of the Telephone*, writes of one such lawsuit filed in 1878 by a professor at Tufts College, Amos E. Dolbear.

"In the course of the Dolbear lawsuit, a Reis machine was brought into court, and created much amusement. It was able to squeak, but not to speak. Experts and professors wrestled with it in vain. It refused to transmit one intelligible sentence. 'It *can* speak, but it *won't*,' explained one of Dolbear's lawyers."[3] Casson's description of the courtroom scene makes it sound as though the lawyer thought the offending instrument was simply behaving as a petulant child might.

Dolbear's suit was not successful.

Alexander Graham Bell would eventually successfully defend his patent against almost six hundred lawsuits. This tells us something about the corruption in the patent office, something about the importance of having good legal counsel when embroiled in a business dispute, and possibly even something about the origins of who invented the telephone.

For what it's worth, my view is that the telephone was actually invented by Jean-François Sudre, a French writer and composer, in the 1820s. Sudre's "Telephone" was a method of communication (also known as Solresol) rather than a device, and it used no electricity, but it is a delightful enough creation that it bears mentioning.

Sudre developed a system of communicating entirely through music by assigning a meaning to each diatonic note of a scale over a three-octave range. Although this did not provide the ability to utilize every letter of the alphabet, it proved to be more than enough to effectively transmit language over a greater distance than is possible through ordinary speech.

Sudre even wrote an entire dictionary of these note-letters, which he was working on until his death, after which his widow completed the task. The dictionary gives the musical notation for how to communicate such disparate phrases as "beef steak" and "constitutional government."[4] Sudre intended for the dictionary to be translated into twelve languages, and he would likely have been disappointed (and we might be surprised) to learn that the work was eventually completed for eight languages. The language received assistance from other sources as well, and an entire grammar, written by a fellow named Boleslas Gajewski, was published in 1902.

Sudre's Telephone did arouse a good deal of interest during his lifetime. At one point it even seemed likely that it would be used by the entire French military,[5] and it was championed by such luminaries as Victor Hugo. But the system was never widely adopted, in part because it required that both parties possess an improbably high level of musical skill. Any attempt to communicate with someone who had less than perfect pitch had the potential for a great deal of confusion: one nineteenth-century observer noted that the musical phrase meaning "to sneeze" meant "manure" when it was played at a slightly higher pitch.[6]

Undeterred by the public's resistance to the invention, Sudre spent decades giving demonstrations of his system. In a combination of concert, magic show, and sales pitch, Sudre would elicit phrases from his captivated audience, writing them down on a piece of paper. He would then translate these words into music and play them for his assistant (who was out of normal speaking range), and the assistant would—ta-da!—write down the phrases verbatim on a blackboard. The crowds ate it up.

Over the years Sudre's Telephone appeared many times to be on the verge of acceptance. He gave demonstrations to great acclaim at the Universal Exhibition in Paris and the London Exhibition, as well as before the king and queen of England and the emperor and empress of France. The average nonmusical person might have difficulty learning it, but the military remained interested due to its great potential for communicating directives and orders over a distance. But ultimately Sudre's Telephone was overtaken by newer artificial languages, such as Volapük and Esperanto, and inventions such as the telegraph somewhat obviated the need for another method of communicating from afar.

*　*　*

It is appealing to consider how our lives might have been different if this strange notion had caught on. Although it would have been difficult to learn Sudre's system, it is not inconceivable. After all, there are numerous tonal languages—such as most of the Chinese dialects, and Hausa, a language spoken in sub-Saharan Africa—in which word meaning changes based on pitch. Recent research has shown that some speakers of tonal languages exhibit a far greater ability to perfectly identify pitch than do speakers of nontonal languages;[7] perhaps if the Telephone language had caught on, we would all be hurtling toward a greater musical understanding.

A number of groups have the ability to communicate through whistling (some linguists estimate that a few hundred whistled languages exist today). Silbo Gomero, a whistling language that corresponds to Castilian Spanish, is still "spoken" by some inhabitants of the Canary Islands. If they can whistle their way through communication, couldn't we have adopted Sudre's musical language?

Although most of us would doubtless have had trouble "speaking" in Telephone, had it lasted, there was one man who would have unquestionably been able to, but he has unfortunately already passed away. And he had such a love for the telephone we use today that it seems unlikely he would ever have changed his allegiance. I am speaking, of course, of the man named Joybubbles.

Joybubbles was blind from birth and gifted with an IQ of 172, perfect pitch, and phenomenal whistling ability. He was born Joe Engressia, a name he retained until 1991, when he changed it to the considerably more descriptive Joybubbles, a name that he thought would make people smile. He was possibly the most accomplished member of a strange and largely forgotten tribe known as "phone phreaks," who may be viewed as the predecessors of today's computer hackers.

Phone phreaks hacked into telephone lines by simulating the tones that phone systems used to communicate to one another. There were several ways of doing this, although Joybubbles adopted the one that would be impossible to replicate without his extremely special abilities—he would whistle into the telephone and trick it into thinking that he was another telephone.

Before he was ten years old, Joybubbles had already discovered that he could fool a telephone into automatically disconnecting by whistling a pitch that would oscillate at exactly 2,600 cycles per second. Before long, he had learned how to whistle the correct pitches that would enable him to make long-distance calls to anywhere in the world.

Phone companies stopped using the tone-based system in the mid-1970s, although by that time Joybubbles had already given up on filching free calls with his whistling (although he continued to be obsessed with the telephone). It is tempting to imagine so gifted a listener and whistler communicating in Sudre's Telephone through the means of Bell's (or Gray's) telephone.

Sudre's system did retain enough appeal that through the beginning of the twentieth century it still had vocal supporters. It seems rather a shame that now, a century later, it has passed away so completely. It has been estimated that between one and two million people continue to speak Esperanto today. Could we not spare a few thousand of them to learn Telephone?

Some small part of me will forever wonder what this language would sound like, and whether a Telephone translation of Goethe's *Sorrows of Young Werther* would sound sadder and more magnificent than a translation of, say, *Marley and Me*.

Another sort of telephone was developed in the early 1840s, also preceding by a few decades the quotidian one that is both a blessing and a plague upon our daily existence. And this one was an actual device rather than a system of language.

John Taylor, a captain in the British navy, invented a communication device that was described in 1845 in *The Year-Book of Facts in Science and Art* as a "powerful instrument for conveying signals during foggy weather."[8] It was capable of producing sounds heard up to six miles away. This modest (although loud) invention appears not to have brought much fame to its creator. For although there are thirty-three John Taylors listed in the *Oxford Dictionary of National Biography*, he is not among them.

The *Oxford Dictionary of National Biography* (*ODNB*) is one of those intellectual and cultural institutions, much like the *Oxford English Dictionary*, that the English are so very good at producing. At 317 pounds and 61,792 pages, the *ODNB* manages to cover an extraordinary amount of biographical information relating to almost anyone of importance connected with the British Isles.

When one searches for a name in the online version of the *ODNB*, it very helpfully lists all the people by that name that it provides a biographical sketch for, and it follows each of these names with a brief description of what the person in question was well known for. Considering that among the plethora of John Taylors, three have merited inclusion in this mighty reference work for being a "friend of Samuel Johnson," a "button manufacturer," and an "itinerant oculist," it would seem that being an early inventor of a device known as the telephone is not as impressive as one might think.

The *ODNB* even has entries for individuals who are described in their occupation simply as "wastrel," such as Frederick William John Augustus Hervey, the seventh marquess of Bristol. Hervey produced very little in life, aside from a seemingly bottomless supply of ill will toward himself*—he certainly never created a telephone—yet he is awarded an entry in the *ODNB*, and John Taylor, the inventor of a useful and noisy maritime device, is not.

Still, John Taylor was an inventor of sorts, and even if his telephone did not have a revolutionary effect on society, I am sure that it had a great impact on some individuals (particularly those at sea in a thick fog).

There were still other forms of telephones that certainly predated Bell's, including such specimens as Francis Whishaw's gutta-percha telephone, which he demonstrated at the London Exhibition of 1851. Gutta-percha is a natural form of rubber, used in insulating telegraph wires, and Whishaw's telephone was able to transmit a whispered conversation over a distance of three-quarters of a mile. But neither Whishaw's nor any of these other early-nineteenth-century devices were truly revolutionary,

---

* The *ODNB* amusingly describes his existence thusly: "His chief occupations were building up his millions in oil, shipping, and property deals and dissipating them in cocaine, heroin, fast cars, rent boys, and a large retinue of camp followers."

at least not revolutionary in the same way that the telephone of today was.

I mention these earlier telephones primarily to illustrate that much of what we think we know about telephone history (when we think of it at all) is vague and incorrect. For instance, most people, when asked when the first wireless telephones (the predecessor to today's unfortunately ubiquitous cellular phones) were in use, would hazard a guess that it was at some point in the mid to late twentieth century. In fact, Alexander Graham Bell developed a way of communicating speech wirelessly in 1880, by transmitting it along waves of light reflected between two large silver discs coated in selenium.

An article in the London *Times* at the time, with the headline "Professor Bell's 'Photophone,'" allowed that the invention "may or may not have any immediate practical application," but still thought it was a very exciting idea.[9] Bell himself appeared to have created the wireless phone simply to show that it could be done, and having demonstrated that two people could talk, without wires, over a distance of several hundred yards, he did not spend much additional time pursuing the matter.

As for the history of long-distance communication before these telephonic devices, there is much evidence of ancient scientific ingenuity applied to communicating over distances. Thousands of years ago the ancient Greeks used a system of torches, arranged to replicate their alphabet, for sending messages over a much farther distance than voice would permit.

Similarly, carrier pigeons have been used for thousands of years as a means of sending messages, as attested to by Ovid's description of the purple-stained bird sent by Taurosthenes to his father, informing him of victory at the Olympic Games. The use of smoke signals, by the American Indians and numerous other groups, obviously predates any form of electric communication by at least a number of centuries. But although these methods of communication fall into the same general category as the telephone, none of them, so far as I am aware, had a book to go with them (with the possible exception of Sudre's dictionary).

The February 21, 1878, issue of the *Yale News* (the first student newspaper in America, and two cents a copy at the time) is four pages long—two of articles and two of advertisements.[10] Some of the articles are more or less similar to what you would see in any of a number of college newspapers published today. There is an editorial on the front page decrying the lack of consistency in senior scientific appointments at the school.

And then some of the articles are simply incomprehensible to most readers of today, due to shifting cultural tides of a hundred and some years. Such would describe the article that ends with the sentence "About ten minutes after the waltzing began, Dr. Skinner appeared and assumed control of the banger, remarking, 'I take this banger away from the *crowd*.'"

The two pages of advertisements look not so different from the advertisements of many other times and places and distinguish themselves mainly through a rather liberal use of the exclamation mark (Nobby Ulsters! Gas Fixtures! Redcliffe's Restaurant! Devoe's Oil!).

Some of the advertisements are for the commonplace needs of students, such as the one Edward P. Judd took out to shill his services as a bookseller and stationer: "The Cheap Book Store!"

Others are geared toward the needs of student and nonstudent alike, such as the ad placed by Gallagher, an importer who was of the opinion that if one exclamation mark per sentence was enticing, then two must be irresistible.

And there was this:

The Greatest Thing Out! TELEPHONE!

This superlative-laced ad goes on to explain that this new-fangled device "can make connections with anyone else having instrument in the city, and can converse with them independent of office. The number of Telephones out is already large, and each day increasing."

The number of telephones may have been increasing each day, but it was far from large. We know this because February 21, 1878, was also the day the first telephone book was released.

Actually, it wasn't a book. And it had no telephone numbers. Yet despite the lack of these salient characteristics, this edition is still widely viewed as the first telephone book.

At first glance it might seem odd that New Haven, with a population at the time of approximately 150,000, would be the home of the first example of this accoutrement to the new technology. But it does make sense, for the very simple reason that it was already the home of one of the world's earliest telephone exchanges, the District Telephone Company of New Haven.

This Connecticut company was not the first business to use telephones. Roswell C. Downer, a Massachusetts banker, rented a pair of them on May 1, 1877, for use as a private line between his home and his office, a distance of three miles.

Isaac Smith set up a switchboard on May 17 of that year for the purpose of having lines connecting doctors with his drugstore. In less than a year's time, this small exchange would prove how useful the telephone could be in an emergency, when a train on the Connecticut Western Railroad crashed and Smith's telephone was used to wake and summon twenty-one doctors to help the victims.

A handful of burglar alarm companies in Boston had telephone exchanges in use before 1878, such as the Holmes Burglar Alarm Company, located at 342 Washington Street, which had launched its switchboard in May 1877. There is no record of whether it had a telephone book of any sort, but another company, Stearns & George (burglar alarm telegraph constructors), had a telephone list dated July 11, 1877, seven months before the exchange in New Haven was open for business. This list was printed by hand, and at the top of the first page it reads, "Memo of Telephone lines in use in Boston and vicinity."[11]

It may be a stretch to say that the small Stearns & George list does in fact constitute the world's first telephone book, but it is not totally implausible. Neither this specimen nor the one found in New Haven the next year had any telephone numbers attached to it, and certainly neither was an actual book, as we commonly define that object. The main claim to primacy that the New Haven directory would appear to have rests on the basis that the listings were printed rather than handwritten, and that eleven of the fifty were for private residences. However, it seems a bit like quibbling to say that this New Haven specimen was only the first telephone "list" or "sheet" for an exchange that was not purely made up of business lines, and thus it's fair to consider it the first actual telephone book.

* * *

The District Telephone Company of New Haven was founded by three men: George W. Coy, Walter Lewis, and Herrick P. Frost. Coy was a disabled veteran of the Civil War, a former telegraph operator for the local offices of the Franklin and the Atlantic and Pacific Telegraph companies, and the inventor of the world's first commercial switchboard. He had long had the dream of opening a telephone company, but he was too poor to do it entirely on his own. So he joined forces with Frost, and the two men borrowed six hundred dollars from Frost's brother-in-law, Walter Lewis. Coy mailed a thousand copies of an advertising circular to the citizens of New Haven, touting the many potential benefits of the new technology. From these thousand letters he received one subscription, from Reverend John E. Todd, a local pastor.

Not a man to give up in the face of this initial adversity, Coy next hired a team of salesmen, who had substantially more luck in drumming up customers. Each salesman was paid $1.50 for every customer he signed up, and in short order they had corralled twenty more customers who were willing to pay for telephone service. Coy began installing telephones in November 1877, with the intention of opening his exchange the following month. He was prevented from doing so by technical difficulties, but he did manage to open the exchange soon after; and by the end of January 1878, the world's first commercial telephone exchange was in operation.

This company bore very little resemblance to even the smallest of the telecommunications firms that would be its eventual descendants in the years to come. The telephone lines were strung up in a slapdash and haphazard fashion, attached to roofs, trees, or almost anything else that would allow them to connect one point to another.

There was almost no furniture in the offices where the telephone exchange was located. A kitchen table held the switchboard that the calls were routed through. Coy, who designed and built the switchboard himself (it was laughingly referred to as "Coy's chicken"),* sat at the table on a soapbox, which served as his desk chair. The office desk was a packing box. An old armchair for visitors rounded out the rest of the furnishings. According to the company records from the time, the total estimated value of all the office goods, including the furniture and the switchboard, was $39.50.

This was an inauspicious beginning for a company that would be the leader in many aspects of American telecommunications. The District Telephone Company of New Haven would become the Southern New England Telephone Company (SNET) in 1882, and in addition to having the world's first commercial telephone exchange and telephone book, it was also responsible for the world's first telephone booth (opened on April 15, 1878), the first coin-operated telephone (1879), and the first school for telephone operators in the nation (March 1907).

But at the beginning of 1878, few of the future glories of this company or of the telephone industry were obvious. When the District Telephone Company's first telephone book was released in February, it spoke of the industry's humble roots: it held fifty

---

* The name, which came about from the odd cackle the switchboard made, was used locally. Elsewhere it was known as "Watson's buzzer," after Thomas Watson, Bell's partner, who had come up with a design for a switchboard.

names, none of which had an accompanying telephone number and several of which were misspelled.

The New Haven telephone directory was not unusual for not having numbers: no exchange would use those for another year, and no telephone book in Connecticut would have them until 1889.[12] The directory existed mainly to alert subscribers to the identities of other telephone owners. Presumably these early subscribers spent time riffling through the pages (or page, if one can riffle a single page), pondering whose day they would intrude upon, and then, upon finding the proper candidate, picking up the telephone. When the operator came on the line, our subscriber would tell him (all of the early telephone operators were men) whom he wanted to pester that day.

At the top of the New Haven directory were the words "List of Subscribers," followed by the company name, address (219 Chapel Street), and date (February 21, 1878). Below that were two columns, listing the fifty locations where a telephone could be found. In addition to the three physicians who subscribed, phones were placed with two dentists, eleven residences, two boarding stables, twenty stores and factories, four meat and fish markets, and eight places marked "Miscellaneous." At the bottom of the sheet it stated, "Office open from 6 a.m. to 2 a.m. After March 1st, this Office will be open all night."[13]

And that was the entirety of the first telephone book.

Although there are many reprints of this ur–telephone directory, there appears to be only one surviving specimen of the "book" itself, and it is located at the Thomas J. Dodd Research Center at the University of Connecticut. The paucity of surviving copies should not be surprising, as the nascent phone company printed only approximately 150 of these initial telephone directories.[14]

Even though there is but one surviving copy, the first telephone book has fared far better than the first telephone exchange itself. This seminal piece of American business history, located at the intersection of State and Chapel streets, was awarded landmark status in 1964, a fairly meaningless honorific that did not prevent the New Haven Redevelopment Agency from tearing it down in 1973 to create a parking garage.[15]

If you ever happen across another one in a thrift store, or tucked away in the pages of some newer telephone book, you would do well to grab hold of it, as it is certainly worth a great deal of money. A slightly newer version of this telephone book, issued by the Connecticut District Telephone Company in New Haven in November 1878, was auctioned by Christie's in May 2008. The book (and it was about twenty pages long, so we may properly call it a book) stated on the front page that it was volume 1, number 1, even though it was certainly not the first such book. Released a mere ten months after the exchange had begun, the number of subscribers had already grown from 50 to 391. Numbers were still not included, although addresses were.

It sold for $170,500. Not bad for a book that is not even a first edition.

This New Haven book had considerably more information in its front matter as to how this devilish new technology should be used. There were admonitions to restrict calls to three minutes at a time and to not use the telephone more than twice in an hour without first getting permission from the central office. Profanity and improper language across the wires was officially frowned upon and "should be reported to this office immediately." In addition to general information on how to use the device and guidelines of propriety, there was an explanation of what to say to the person on the other end of the telephone line. The proper way to begin a telephone conversation, the book exhorted, was with a firm and cheery "Hulloa."[16]

Telephonic Greetings

"Hello," as a greeting, seems as long-standing as the English language itself, and one can easily imagine that it was in use back when our linguistic ancestors were still living in mud huts and pestering the Romans. Incredibly, the advent of the telephone seems to mark the beginning of a great surge in this word's popularity in our language.

The word "hello" as a greeting predates the telephone (the *Oxford English Dictionary* gives the first recorded use of it in 1827), but it was generally not used in such a widespread fashion. The word was more often used as a means of attracting someone's attention ("Hello, what do you think you're doing?") or to express some form of mild surprise ("Hello, what have we here?"). An editorial aside in the same dictionary states that "Thomas Edison is popularly credited with instigating the practice of saying 'hello' when answering the telephone . . . and for the word's subsequent popularity as a greeting. His rival, Alexander Graham Bell, preferred 'ahoy' to be used." (Indeed, Bell insisted on answering the phone with "ahoy" for all the rest of his days.)

No matter whether one prefers Bell's "ahoy" or Edison's

"hello," we should all be grateful that it was one of these mercifully succinct phrases that caught on, and not one of the other opening lines that were common among people who were first getting acquainted with the telephone: "Do I get you?" and "Are you there?" were options at the time.

According to family lore, I was about six years old when I first began to answer the telephone at home. I do not have any specific recollection of this, but the story has stayed with me because my parents are so fond of repeating it. In what was to be an apt foreshadowing of my utter lack of future social graces, I would hurry to the telephone when it rang, place it to my ear, and immediately adopt the interrogative voice, saying, "What?" If only I had a copy of an early telephone book to guide me in etiquette (or parents who were more concerned with whether or not I offended callers), I might have learned that the proper way to answer the telephone is with a firm and clear "hello" (or "hulloa").

It is a curious thing that we should have so readily adopted "hello" as a means of greeting rather than "ahoy." While the latter may have lost ground due to the fact that it was primarily a nautical greeting, it had been in use for some time longer than "hello," dating in print to the middle of the eighteenth century and likely used in speech for considerably longer.

Regardless of which side of the "ahoy" vs. "hello" debate you come down on, I hope we can all agree that it's too bad that another of the recommendations of the November 1878 telephone directory has not survived to the present day: the book advised that the proper way to end a conversation was with the phrase "That is all."

This strikes me as an eminently more honest and forthright way to end a phone call than "good-bye." "Good-bye," "bye-bye," and all the other variants are ultimately contractions of the phrase "God be with you" (or "with ye"). I don't know about you, but I don't really mean to say that when I end a conversation. I suppose I could say "ciao"—which does have a certain Continental flair to it . . . but also the unfortunate etymological background of coming from the Italian *schiavo*, which means "I am your slave," and I don't much want to say that either. "Cheerio," "pip-pip," "toodle-oo," "ta-ta," and any number of other silly things that one could say at the end of a conversation (and some do) are all of some uncertain origin, imitative, or simply nonsense words.

We have overlooked a wonderfully declarative way to end a conversation. You have said what you intended to say, you now have nothing else to declare, and so you finish your speech without any evangelical flourishes, blandishments you don't mean, or childish prattle—"That is all."

For several decades the great newscaster Walter Cronkite would end his broadcasts by saying "And that's the way it is," a fine turn of phrase that has almost as much pith and truth to it as "That is all." Broadcast journalist Linda Ellerbee had a similar method of ending her news segments, with the trenchant "And so it goes." These are perfectly serviceable phrases, but even they don't have the clarity and utility of "That is all." I should like to see "That is all" make a comeback in colloquial speech, and I have resolved to attempt to adopt it in the few telephone conversations that I engage in.

Although we hear the phrase far more rarely than was suggested by the early telephone books of New Haven, "That is all" was not completely lost. A number of police departments adopted the use of this phrase when signing off, not on the telephone but over the airwaves. The standard method of employing it was to say

"That is all," followed by the name of the officer who was making the broadcast. An example of this may be heard in the 1944 cartoon "Donald Duck and the Gorilla," in which the details of the escape from a local zoo by the titular gorilla is announced over the police scanner by a disembodied voice, which continually throughout the episode says the phrase "That is all . . . Breckenridge."

Even though "hello" was recommended as the preferred method of greeting when speaking to a person who answered the telephone once the call was put through, it was soon discouraged as a greeting when used by the operators themselves, as it was seen as a potential way to initiate conversation with callers, which was greatly frowned upon. When the telephone company in Connecticut began listing its patrons by number, approximately a decade after service began, it instituted a policy requiring all operators to answer the line with the stark and impersonal "What number?"

Some operators preferred to answer the line in what they thought was a more human fashion and were resistant to making this switch in greeting. The general superintendant of the company sent the operators a sternly worded letter in 1892, making it clear that such frivolity would not be tolerated: "I notice that *some* operators, either carelessly or willfully, are continually violating the rule of the Company."[17]

It may be difficult to imagine now, but it was once possible to have some small amount of prestige as a result of being in the telephone book—if you were the last surviving member of the first one ever.

By 1933, Dr. Ernest LeRoy Thomson was the last remaining member of the original subscribers listed in the very first

New Haven telephone book. Dr. Thomson was a young doctor practicing in New Haven when the telephone was first offered. Although more than a dozen physicians lived in the city at the time, Thomson, an 1874 graduate of Yale, was one of only three that consented to have a home telephone—the others all thought it would be bad for their health to have patients calling them at home in the evenings.

Dr. Thomson was forward-thinking in other ways: he was one of the first Americans to embrace the newfangled life insurance policies that were just beginning to be offered in the late nineteenth century; he was one of the first in his area to purchase and use an automobile; and as a physician he was known for his habit of creating and assigning diet lists to his patients, a practice that met with varied success among the New Haven residents of the day.

Thomson had been the subject of some controversy earlier in life—he was expelled from the New Haven Medical Association in 1883 for his alleged role in helping a woman procure an abortion.[18] By the time of his death, this episode appears to have been largely forgotten; in his obituary, the *New York Times* described him as "one of the most successful general practitioners in the state."[19]

At the time of his death, in 1934, Dr. Thomson had had continuous telephone service for over fifty-six years, a fact that was apparently regarded as somewhat more of an accomplishment at the time than it might be today, as evidenced by the fact that he received numerous messages congratulating him on being the longest-running subscriber. Proud of his association with the telephone until the very end of his life, Dr. Thomson kept a photograph of the 1878 directory tacked to the wall next to his bed.

2

"IT TALKS!"

The U.S. Patent Office (USPO) awarded 182,928 patents in 2007, followed by 185,244 in 2008. In 2009, the inventors of the world, or at least the United States, ratcheted up their productivity and were awarded a staggering 191,947 patents.

If one chooses to read through the patents granted (and, I have to say, this is reading I can highly recommend—you will likely not find any material that is quite so humorous, sad, and odd as the claims of what many of these patents will achieve for humanity), one is struck not only by the number of inventions but by the number of failed inventions. We are constantly coming up with ideas that never quite catch on.

Many of these failed ideas happen to fail for a very good reason—they are terrible ideas. One need look no further than the patents awarded for such inventions as the Lap-Dance Liner

(U.S. Patent #RE39,371), the butter-stick slicer (#D551,917), or the "flossing kit for cleaning pierced body parts" (#7,083,602).

Some of the almost two hundred thousand patents awarded every year are doubtless going to save lives or at least improve them in some measurable sense. But the vast majority of the rest are nothing more than minor adjustments to something that very few of us will ever hear of, such as a new form of cotter pin or an adjustment to some cathode ray. Another large number of the patents awarded appear to be little more than the cheap plastic simulacrum of intellectual innovation. I cannot help but wonder if somewhere an incorporeal landfill is being stuffed to overflow by these ideas, or if the capacity for intellectual waste is infinite.

Some inventions have had an immediate and obvious use, such as the nuclear bomb. Its utility (that is, its capacity to kill large numbers of people) may have been a terrible one, but it was no less obvious for it. Penicillin, on the other hand, had an equally immediate and obvious utility—it could save people who would otherwise have died from infection. The vast majority of inventions one comes across, however, do not have the immediate and obvious use that a powerful bomb or drug has. In fact, many of them leave one scratching the head to try to figure out what they are useful for.

The telephone (U.S. Patent #174465) may not have fallen into the same category (soul-wrenching uselessness) as the pointless patents mentioned previously, but it was still not guaranteed instant success. There is a fair amount of precedent for devices that are largely ignored when they are first released yet eventually come to be seen as indispensable. When the dishwasher was inflicted upon the American public in the early part of the twentieth century, it was not at all the smashing success that its manufacturers thought it would be. Surprised, the dishwasher makers took a poll of housewives and found that many of them considered washing dishes to be among the least onerous of their chores, and they didn't much mind washing the dishes by hand. And so a campaign was launched to convince people that having a dishwasher was a luxury rather than a necessity. The effort was quite successful, and the dishwasher soon made the transition from newfangled item viewed with suspicion to nearly ubiquitous necessity.

Another device that had a slow start was one much closer to the telephone: its immediate predecessor, the telegraph. Few people had ever seen anything like the telegraph before. To be sure, there were other ways of communicating over a great distance—semaphores, carrier pigeons, smoke signals, and the like—but this device, on which one tapped in a seemingly foreign code, must have seemed like magic. Perhaps that was the problem; the telegraph may well have been so fantastic that few believed it was real.

The very first day the telegraph was open for business and charging money for the service of communicating with a faraway station, it managed to take in an entire cent, and the take would have been half as much if there had been change for a penny. The rates for the telegraph were set by the U.S. Postal Service, which decided that it would cost one cent for every four characters sent.

A man from Virginia stopped by and said that he wanted to see the telegraph working, but that he only had two pieces of currency, a penny and a twenty-dollar bill. Rather than break the twenty-dollar bill, he opted to have a short message sent back and forth between Washington, DC, and Baltimore, which consisted of the following exchange:

Washington: 4 (which in telegraph code meant "What time is it?")
Baltimore: 1 (which in telegraph code meant "One.")

Presumably the man was well satisfied by this and went on his way, telling all and sundry of the new wonders of modern communication. And the news spread, but not so rapidly. A week after the exchange was open, it was taking in a profit of about a dollar a day.

But prior to this, a certain amount of deliberation had taken place as to whether the telegraph would be of any real use. Many members of Congress who had been asked to help in funding its research stated emphatically that it would be a waste of both time and money to assist the developers, Samuel Morse and Alfred Vail. And Vail himself, in a letter to his wife during the early days of the telegraph's use, wrote, "I hope the thing will come to something by and by."[1]

One of the electric inventions with perhaps the greatest influence on life in the twentieth century, at least in terms of its social influence, also developed at a considerably different, if not slower, pace than expected: the television.

A watchable form of television was developed in the 1920s. The Scottish inventor John Logie Baird gave a demonstration of it in 1926, when he transmitted images between two rooms in the same building. The next year, AT&T managed to transmit televised moving images from Washington, DC, to New York City. By 1930, laboratories at AT&T had developed a form of two-way video-telephoning in which two people could watch each other as they spoke; service was set up between two locations, 195 Broadway and 463 West Street in New York City.[2]

It was expected that this ability to connect people, so that rather than just talking to another disembodied voice each could actually see the person to whom he or she was speaking, would be a smashing success. The *Bell Telephone Journal* published a cartoon in June 1930 titled "Wait'll we all television," which was a poorly drawn montage of imaginary scenes in the near future, when it was thought that we all would be talking to each other on the television. The television sets in the cartoon of 1930 look exactly like the flat-screen computer monitors of today. Seeing that people can and do talk to each other over the Internet now in just this fashion, it would seem that the prediction did come true, albeit some seventy-five years later than envisioned.

Alexander Graham Bell had just received his patent on the telephone when the 1876 Centennial Exhibition was held in Philadelphia. This was the first time that the exhibition (which would come to be called the World's Fair) was taking place in the United States, and it was a momentous occasion.

The memory of the Civil War was a recent and ugly scar on the image of the nation, and it had been followed by years of political upheaval and corruption. There was still a lingering suspicion among Europeans that the United States was a backwater nation, and so the fair presented a great opportunity to exhibit the growth, both potential and realized, of the country.

In the six months that it was open, the Centennial Exhibition had an estimated nine million visitors—a sizable number, considering that the population of the United States at the time was only about forty-six million.[3] There were exhibits from thirty-seven nations, and many more individual exhibitors were spread among the 250 pavilions on the fairgrounds, a 285-acre tract near the Schuylkill River.

Admission to the fair was fifty cents, and for an additional two quarters visitors could climb a ladder to the balcony at the top of the right arm and torch of the not yet constructed Statue of Liberty. The fair ended up not being a great financial success, although it did perform an admirable job of showcasing the developments, technological and otherwise, of the hundred-year-old nation.

The Corliss Steam Engine, a marvel of nineteenth-century engineering, was shown at the fair and was responsible for providing the power to many of the other machines on exhibit.[4] One of the precursors to the electric light, the Wallace-Farmer Electric Dynamo attracted great excitement, as did the Remington Typographic Machine (soon to be known as the typewriter).

Not all of the exhibits were concerned with technological improvement; some had more to do with gustatory pleasures. Hires Root Beer had a booth at the fair, as did Heinz Ketchup.

One of the most visited pavilions was that of the Turkish delegation. This may have stemmed from a fascination with the martial splendors of the declining Ottoman Empire, or perhaps it was due to the fact that it was at the 1876 exhibition that the Turks purportedly first introduced marijuana to the American public.[5]

The reaction to the exhibition was not one of unanimous approval. In particular, the buildings—most of which were designed by Hermann J. Schwarzmann, a young German architect—were excoriated. In 1931 Lewis Mumford wrote, "It is hard to conceive anything lower than the architecture of the Centennial Exposition."[6] And from the vantage of 1954, the rather strident critic

Russell Lynes, author of *The Taste-Makers*, wrote, "Critics today look back upon the Centennial Exhibition as an architectural and artistic calamity that produced not a single new idea."[7]

But it was still a heady time, the point at which America was leaving the age of steam and entering the age of electricity, and it was just the sort of place where an inventor eager to display his wares proudly to the world would want to show them. Alexander Graham Bell did have a table at the electrical exhibit, but it was not very prominently placed, being underneath a staircase.[8]

Bell had been uncertain as to whether it was even a good idea for him to bring his new, not fully tested telephone to the exhibition. But after much thought, he finally decided to, and he had the good fortune to be underneath his staircase at a fortuitous moment. On June 25, the judges of the exposition were touring the building that housed the electrical exhibits. They were joined by a handful of dignitaries, including the emperor of Brazil, Dom Pedro II, who was known for being considerably more progressive than most of his fellow nineteenth-century emperors (admittedly, he did have to be removed from office through a military coup). But the emperor of Brazil was not prone to some of the imperatorial excesses that were characteristic of his contemporaries, such as whipping peasants until they died. He was also known for his interest in the sciences.

Dom Pedro was acquainted with Bell through his interest in the latter's work with a school for the deaf, so it is not at all surprising that he would have stopped by his booth, even though it was underneath the staircase. He could not, however, have been expecting what he would find there, and it showed in his reaction. He placed the telephone to his ear and, turning to the judges accompanying him, bellowed out what would have been a great advertising catch-phrase for television, if they had need of such things at the time.

"My God, it talks!"

The immediate effect of these four words was that Bell quickly lost his place under the stairs, and he and the telephone were moved to a far more central location in the exhibit.[9] The long-term effects are more difficult to judge with any certainty, but it seems safe to say that these were the most important words spoken into a telephone after its inventor's saying, "Mr. Watson—come here—I want to see you."[*] A story has long been in circulation about an internal memo at Western Union from 1876 that is supposed to indicate the low regard in which the telephone was held at the time that it was first invented. In this tale, a faceless bureaucrat makes what is, in hindsight, one of the worst business decisions of all time in declining to purchase the rights to the telephone. ("This 'telephone' has too many shortcomings to be seriously considered as a means of communication. The device is inherently of no value to us.") The story, like so many of its ilk, is almost certainly false, and no one has ever produced evidence of this damning memo.[†]

---

[*] A minor side note to this phrase, the most famous (and oft-misquoted) of all telephone utterances. Michael Erard, the author of *Um . . . : Slips, Stumbles, and Verbal Blunders, and What They Mean*, points out that the actual first word spoken by Bell in this exchange was "um."

[†] Although there does appear to be credence to the story that Gardiner Greene Hubbard, one of the founders of the Bell Telephone Company, offered to sell the rights to the telephone as an invention to Western Union for the piddling sum of one hundred thousand dollars, an offer that was refused. It is mentioned in the autobiography of Bell's partner, Thomas Watson.

But stories like this, even though they are usually false, often exist for a reason. Much of the country was not yearning for a telephone. And even shortly before the telephone was invented, much of the populace would likely have laughed at the notion that such a thing could be invented. This is evident through a story related by Francis Jehl, Thomas Edison's lab assistant, in his memoirs, *Menlo Park Reminiscences*, wherein he describes an editorial published in the *Boston Herald-News* several years before Bell was awarded his patent for the telephone. The editorialist decries the perniciousness of one Joshua Coppersmith, who had been attempting to hoodwink people on the street into giving him money by hawking a fantastical device that he claimed would allow people to talk to each other over a great distance by communicating through metal wires. He called his device the telephone, a term that the newspaper roundly derided, saying that it was "obviously intended to imitate the word 'telegraph.'"[10]

And even after the telephone had already been invented and publicly demonstrated, there was no public consensus that it could be of any use, and as is so often the case with a misunderstood breakthrough, the typical reaction was that of scorn. In *The History of the Telephone*, Herbert Casson describes some of the vituperation visited upon Bell:

> He was an "impostor," a "ventriloquist," a "crank who says he can talk through a wire." The London *Times* alluded dismissively to the telephone as the latest American humbug, and gave many profound reasons why speech could not be sent over a wire, because of the intermittent nature of the electric

current. "Almost all electricians," the paper chided, "the men who were supposed to know, pronounced the telephone an impossible thing."[11]

Casson also points out that even when people had an opportunity to actually use the telephone, and to see that there was no tiny man hiding inside of it to make it work, there was a discernible lack of enthusiasm. "People who talked for the first time into a telephone box had a sort of stage fright. They felt foolish. To do so seemed an absurd performance, especially when they had to shout at the top of their voices. Plainly, whatever of convenience there might be in this new contrivance was far outweighed by the loss of personal dignity; and very few men had sufficient imagination to picture the telephone as a part of the machinery of their daily work."[12]

As inauspicious as the telephone's beginning was in the United States, it was still far more promising than the response it received in Britain, where it was politely sneered at in the House of Commons during a committee hearing. Sir William Preece, the chief engineer of the General Post Office, was asked about the likelihood of the telephone proving itself as popular or useful as it was in America:

I fancy that the descriptions we get of its use in America are a little exaggerated. . . . Here we have a superabundance of messengers, errand boys, and things of that kind. In America they are wanted, and one of the most striking things to an Englishman there is to see how the Americans have adopted in their houses call bells and telegraphs and telephones, and all kinds of aids to their domestic arrangements, which have been forced upon them by necessity.[13]

I wonder if the number of telephones in Britain today corresponds in any way to the number of "messengers, errand boys, and things of that kind," or if it perhaps instead maps to how much people wanted a telephone.

By the beginning of 1880, there were already 30,000 telephone subscribers in the United States, a number that increased to almost 50,000 by the end of that year. Each year saw the addition of some twenty or thirty thousand new telephone subscribers, so that by the beginning of 1888, just ten years after the first commercial exchange opened in Connecticut, there were almost 160,000 of the instruments merrily ringing in homes and businesses across the land.

So after the initial skepticism, the telephone obviously did catch on with the general American public, and it did so rapidly. But certain portions of the population proved to be recalcitrant when it came to adopting the device. The first American president to have a telephone on his desk was Herbert Hoover, who had one installed in 1929. The White House did have a telephone well before most of the country, as Rutherford B. Hayes had had one installed in the telegraph room of the executive mansion in 1878. It received little use at first, since so few other people had telephones at that time. The very first telephone book for the city of Washington, DC, lists this presidential telephone simply as "No. 1."

Eventually the telephone was moved into the hallway outside the Oval Office; when he needed to make a call, the president would step out of his office to do so. When William Howard Taft was president (1909–13), an extra-large telephone booth was installed in the White House, specially designed to accommodate his rather formidable bulk.[14]

Once it became apparent that the telephone was here with a degree of permanence, its champions began to breathlessly proclaim the marvelous things it would bring about. In an article published in the *Journal of the Telegraph* in May 1880, the telephone was considered something soon to be responsible for nothing short of world peace:

> The result can be nothing less than a new organization of society—a state of things in which every individual, however secluded, will have at call every other individual in the community, to the saving of no end of social and business complications, of needless goings to and fro, of disappointments, delays, and a countless host of those great and little evils and annoyances which go so far under present conditions to make life laborious and unsatisfactory.
>
> The time is close at hand when the scattered members of civilized communities will be as closely united, so far as instant telephonic communication is concerned, as the various members of the body now are by the nervous system.[15,*]

* The claims made about the potential of the telephone may have been hyperbolic, but they were demure compared to those offered by David Sarnoff as he introduced NBC and commercial television to the world at the 1939 World's

Yet, as with any new form of technology, there were those who were convinced that somehow this contraption would cause irreparable damage to the callow fools who fell prey to its wiles. In 1901, the *American Telephone Journal* published an article that quoted an unnamed "specialist" from New Orleans; the article began with the compelling opening line "The telephone habit has become a disease with a great many persons."

This specialist warned of the many minor problems brought about by the telephone, most of which seemed to be connected to the problem of making inappropriate telephone calls when inebriated. But as he warmed to his task, the antitelephone fellow found some other potential harms of the telephone—"the human voice may lose something of its mellowness," "the hearing may be considerably deadened," and, most fearsome of all, "the ear might be flattened out until it would be as smooth as if it had been pressed with a flatiron."

Although he allowed that these changes would take as long as a few centuries to come about, the fact that his thesis could not be proven in his lifetime did not stop the telephone specialist from bringing his fearmongering to a crescendo:

"Just think of the awfulness of the thing! Here is the telephone flattening out the human ear, and on one side of the head at that, robbing the human voice of its mellowness, and deadening the hearing, and there is the bicycle humping the human

---

Fair: "It is with a feeling of humbleness that I come to this moment of announcing the birth in this country of a new art so important in its implications that it is bound to affect all society. It is an art which shines like a torch of hope in a troubled world. It is a creative force which we must learn to utilize for the benefit of all mankind."

back and spraddling the human legs. Really it is not a pretty thing to look at."[16]

Although it quickly became apparent that the telephone was an instrument of great utility and, furthermore, that it would not flatten out the ear of the person using it, this did not mean that it was favored by all. Indeed, soon after the value of the telephone was discovered, so, too, were the myriad annoyances that could be introduced by having possession of a seemingly magic box that could connect people across great distances. In 1888, a subscriber to the Southern New England Telephone Company sent the company a letter, asking that it please come and remove his telephone, as he used it infrequently and other people were constantly coming by to borrow it. "I am tired of supplying an instrument for an entire village."

The peevish letter writer apparently wished to make sure that the telephone company fully understood the reasons for his displeasure, as he went on at some length in the missive, enumerating the reasons that having a telephone was a bother: "The last feather was last evening, when a German came to the house to have my wife telephone to Malony's to remove a dead horse from some place a mile or two away. I am long suffering and extremely patient, but the last was too much, and the telephone must go."[17]

Mark Twain echoed the feelings that many people had for the telephone, although he did so in far wittier fashion than they would have, when his Christmas greetings were published in the *Boston Globe* in 1890: "It is my heart-warm and world-embracing Christmas hope and aspiration that all of us, the high, the low, the rich, the poor, the admired, the despised, the loved, the hated, the civilized, the savage (every man and brother of us all throughout the whole earth), may eventually be gathered together in a heaven of everlasting rest and peace and bliss, except the inventor of the telephone."

Once the telephone caught on, in spite of Twain's antipathy, it was quickly apparent that there was a need for a way of keeping all the different numbers organized, and although the first several telephone books did not actually supply numbers, they did give lists of the other subscribers and provide other useful information, such as how to use the instrument.

That an instrument as common and simple as the telephone needed instructions may come as a surprise, almost as if it turned out that nineteenth-century Americans needed written assistance to put on their hats. But telephones were an entirely new concept, one that most people did not naturally take to. So the early telephone books were used as a means of education; they came with instructions in the front that may seem risible to us today but that were of great use to many people. We may laugh at these instructions now, but they were necessary—there was nothing intuitive about early telephones. A New York City telephone directory from 1885 gave the following instructions:

TO CALL.

Press in the button and turn the crank *once only*; unhook the listening telephone (receiver) and put it close to your ear, when Central Office will enquire: "What number?" Give *Central Office and number* of person wanted, and upon receiving the answer "All right," hang up the receiver, and wait until your bell rings, then place the receiver to your ear and address person called. If you do not immediately hear his voice, the delay—except in rare cases—is owing to his failure to promptly answer the call. Therefore, hang up the receiver, press in the button and ring twice, then put the receiver again to your ear. Speak in a moderate, clear tone, with mouth three or four inches from transmitter. Loud speaking jars the mechanism of the instrument and produces a confused sound. When through do not fail to hang up the receiver, and call off, pressing in button and turning crank *once*. If you wish to call for a subscriber before disconnection is made, hang up your receiver, press in button, and turn crank *once*; then immediately place receiver to your ear and Central Office will answer.

If subscribers will respond quickly when their bells are rung the service will be much improved.

If bell rings *once* pay no attention—you are not wanted. If it rings *twice* you are wanted. Unhook receiver and *speak* immediately. The receiver, except when at your ear, must be *always on the hook*.

Other times, the instructions in the telephone book were more like admonishments to an unruly child than they were an explanation of how to use a brand-new technology. Another telephone book from New York City, also from 1885, has sternly worded marginalia, warning the customer about things they should not do.

Sometimes these warnings enumerate what is and what is not permitted: "If you permit non-subscribers to use this telephone, the Company will raise your rate." Subscribers would be charged an additional five dollars a month if they were found to have illicitly shared their telephone.

But most of the warnings were simply further instructions on how to properly use the new technology. Sometimes it seemed that the telephone company itself had not yet worked out the terminology it would use, as when it warned customers, "When you hear others calling on the 'calling wire,' don't break in; your call cannot be heard." The phrase "calling wire" did not last for very long.

My favorite instructional marginalia from old New York City telephone books are the brusque exhortations at the bottoms of some of the pages from the Metropolitan 1885 directory: "Don't say, 'Hello! Hello, Central!' It won't do any good." And just in case that point has not been made sufficiently clear, later in the book it once again states, "The Operators will not answer or pay any attention to 'Hello! Hello, Central!' or to any other words that are worse than useless." For the benefit of those obviously dense individuals who hadn't yet figured out how to interact with the operators, there is still another reprimand at the bottoms of some of the pages: "The operators are too busy to talk with you; if you have any question to ask, call '525.'" It is easy to imagine that the long-suffering operators were begging for even more such directives in the directories.

We may laugh today at these instructions for how to speak into the telephone or reminders that the telephone must be hung up when finished or admonitions that the operators were not there for chatting. But it is difficult to use any form of new technology, and the telephone certainly qualified as new.

I once had one of these (now old) telephones; it came with an apartment I rented in Brooklyn. It was essentially a handsome and exceedingly large oak box that I found in the basement, dusted off, and screwed to the wall. The wiring had at some point been updated so that it could accommodate a rotary dial, but the rest of the phone had all its original parts. Thus, in order to speak, you would put your face up to the mouthpiece that was in the middle of the box, and all listening was done through the separate, handheld earpiece. Whenever guests would come over, they would want to use this strange-looking telephone. Inevitably they would promptly use it incorrectly, generally by attempting to both talk and listen through the mouthpiece. Old technology can be just as confusing to decipher as new.

I used this telephone for a few weeks, until I made the fateful error of attempting to mix nineteenth-century technology with that of the twenty-first. When I plugged the telephone into the VoIP (Voice over Internet Protocol) box I had, it stubbornly refused to make any more calls.

Keeping in Touch

What did people do before they had telephones? How did they ask after their relative who was in the hospital—indicating sufficient familial concern that they would ask after the health of a cousin, but not so much that they would pay him a visit? How did they communicate that they would be ten minutes later than they had thought they would be? How did they engage in meaningless conversation with someone who lived far away? These may seem like odd questions to ask today, in an era in which so many people can always be reached through a splendid (some would say strangling) network of cellular phones, instant messaging, and email. But not so very long ago the ways of getting in touch with someone entailed practices that are almost entirely foreign to us now, or that appear to be headed the way of the dodo and the hand-delivered milk bottle.

The most obvious method of getting a message to a distant person in the days before the telephone existed would be to send a letter through the U.S. mail. In the 1870s, letters were relatively inexpensive to send, just two cents an ounce,[18] and postcards could be sent for a penny.

Paper mail may have been inexpensive to send, but it had the drawback of being a relatively slow form of communication. By the middle of the nineteenth century, one could send mail from the east coast to the west, but the estimated time of delivery was three to four weeks, although shipments (usually sent via steamship) were known on occasion to take months to arrive.[19] A month! Think of all the things that could happen in that time span; today when we look over the news of thirty days ago, it seems as though it were from some distant time and place.

Another problem with sending information by mail in the 1870s was that almost one-fifth of the U.S. population was illiterate.[20] It wouldn't much matter how fast or slow your letter arrived if the recipient could not read it.

There were few faster options for sending an actual paper letter through the mails. The fabled Pony Express, the first express mail service in America, only operated for about a year and a half, from April 1860 until October of the following year. This early version of rush delivery relied on a network of dozens of riders and hundreds of horses. A rider would travel a distance of seventy-five to one hundred miles at a time, changing horses every ten to fifteen miles.

This service was considerably more expensive than the regular mail—a half-ounce letter could cost as much as five dollars to send. It did have the advantage of (relative) expediency—the two-thousand-mile trip from St. Joseph, Missouri, the westernmost point that the telegraphs and railroads reached at the time, to Sacramento, California, was usually covered in ten days. The fastest delivery that ever occurred on that route was the seven days and seventeen hours it took to deliver a copy of Abraham Lincoln's inaugural address in 1861. When the transcontinental telegraph was completed in late 1861, the Pony Express became just another outdated form of communication, and heavily in debt, it folded.[21]

When the telephone made its debut, the possibility of sending letters by air was still decades away (the U.S. Postal Service did not begin using airplanes until 1911), and even when this form of expedited delivery began, many people were reluctant to use it because it was more expensive than regular mail.[22]

Throughout the last two hundred years, the mail has moved by train, ship, horse, coach, plane, motorcycle, and truck. As time has progressed, the postal service has continually found faster and more reliable methods of getting the mail from one place to another, yet none of the methods ever approached the speed with which a telegraph or telephone call could transmit information. With one notable and short-lived exception: sending the mail by missile.

For a brief and gloriously odd period of time from the late nineteenth through the middle of the twentieth century, there was a belief that missiles could be used for something other than inflicting damage on property and person. Instead, someone had the bright idea that the power of projectile ballistics should be harnessed to bring people together rather than to blow them to pieces. In particular, missiles, it was suggested, might greatly facilitate the speed at which mail was sent. In 1870, during the Prussian siege of Paris, a Frenchman by the name of J. D. Schneiter applied for a patent to send mail out of the besieged city by rocket. By the time his patent application was granted, on February 9 of the next year, the siege had been lifted and there was no pressing need to send mail via rocket. There is no evidence that Schneiter ever followed through on this plan.

Decades later, Friedrich Schmiedl and Gerhard Zucker, an Austrian and a German rocket scientist, conducted a number of experiments (many of which were successful) in sending mail via rocket, in the years between 1928 and 1936. But the first true mail sent between post offices in this bombastic fashion in the United States was on February 23, 1936, when two bags of letters were hurtled across two thousand feet of frozen lake between the towns of Greenwood Lake, New York, and Hewitt, New Jersey. The rocket did not make it all the way across—it crashed on the way—but it had enough momentum to continue skittering across the ice to the other side, where the postmaster of Hewitt obligingly picked up the mail sacks and dragged them into the post office.

The enthusiasm for sending mail by missile appears to have dimmed for a while after this experiment, although the U.S. Postal Service had unrealized plans to send the mail across Niagara Falls. However, soon enough the inherent and touchingly naïve human faith that implements of destruction will inevitably lead to the betterment of the world prevailed, and in 1959 the postal service once again embraced the idea of bombing people with mail. On June 8 of that year, under the aegis of Postmaster General Arthur E. Summerfield, a Regulus missile loaded with letters was launched from the USS *Barbero* (a submarine whose name was a synonym for the surgeonfish) one hundred miles off the Florida coast.

The epistolary missile in question, the Regulus, was operated by remote control and was capable of speeds of six hundred miles an hour. It took approximately twenty-two minutes for the mail to fly the one hundred miles from the USS *Barbero* to the Mayport Naval Auxiliary Air Station.

The missile carried three thousand letters, and according to a *New York Times* article the next day, every single one of them was written by the postmaster general. The letters, addressed to President Eisenhower and a host of government officials, were then sent from the nearby Jacksonville Post Office by more conventional means. No mention was made of how the postmaster general found the time to write three thousand letters.

All of these letters were enclosed in special commemorative envelopes, and each one was emblazoned with the words "First Official Missile Mail." The earlier attempts of the 1930s were apparently deemed not historic enough to count, as no mention was made of them.*

Postmaster Summerfield was exceedingly keen on the idea of sending the mail via missiles. He was quoted as saying, "Before

---

* Anyone who cares to find out more about the peculiar practice of sending mail by rocket should consult the work *Rocket Mail Flights of the World to 1986*, by Max Kronstein.

man reaches the moon, mail will be delivered within hours from New York to California, to England, to India or to Australia by guided missile."[23]

Needless to say, the practice of sending mail by rocket never enjoyed the success that Summerfield had hoped for, and the whole episode has now become just an interesting side note in the history of how mail was sent.

In the meantime, if one wanted to get in touch with someone and didn't want to wait the time that was required by most forms of the mail, there was the telegraph. Telegraphing was not nearly as cheap as sending a letter (sending a ten-word message from New York to Chicago in 1870 cost a dollar),[24] but it did have the advantage of being virtually instantaneous.

The telegraph was still a relatively recent invention at the time that the telephone made its debut; it was developed in the late 1830s, and the ability to send a message from one side of the country to the other was not realized for more than twenty years. It took a few decades to build and set up the nationwide network of wires and cables that would allow transmission of messages across thousands of miles.

The question of who invented the telegraph cannot be answered fully, as the device came about through the work of a number of inventors during a period of well over a hundred years. One thing that does appear relatively certain is that, traditional wisdom notwithstanding, Samuel Morse was not the inventor.

In 1729 in England, a former dyer and a member of the Royal Society named Stephen Gray, with the help of his friend

Granville Wheeler, discovered how to send an electrical signal through more than eight hundred feet of wire, making a feather at the end move. In 1787, a French philosopher and scientist named Lomond sent coded electrical messages a short distance over a wire to his wife.

In America as well, Morse had predecessors. The owner of a racetrack on Long Island, Harrison Gray Dyar, had developed a method of sending messages over a three-mile length of wire that he ringed around his racetrack. Shortly after developing this method of sending information, Dyar was falsely accused of spying and opted to leave the country. He lived for most of the rest of his life in London and Paris; managed to accumulate a substantial fortune through other, nontelegraphic inventions; and returned to live in New York at the end of his life.

Dyar may not have invented the very first telegraph, but it is likely that no one in America had a working model before he did. And so it seems rather unfair that he should be so entirely overlooked as an inventor. To the extent that he is mentioned in history books or encyclopedias, it is usually only in the context that he was the father of Harrison Gray Dyar Jr., a brilliant entomologist who was one of the world's foremost authorities on mosquitoes, but was himself mostly known for his purported bigamy, adherence to the Baha'i faith, and the fact that he had the peculiar habit of digging a series of tunnels in his backyard that extended for hundreds and hundreds of feet. After digging these tunnels, all very neatly ordered and six by six feet, he would line them with brick. When these tunnels were discovered in 1924 after a truck fell into one of them, there was speculation that they were the work of spies from World War I or else reclusive scientists. No one seemed inclined to believe Dyar's contention that he dug them to relax himself.[25]

Samuel Morse (along with Alfred Vail) did indeed develop the first commercially viable telegraph in the United States. Most of us have a dim memory of learning at some point around eighth grade that he also sent the very first telegraph, composed of the weighty and portentous phrase "What hath God wrought?"

These four words, burned into the memory of countless schoolchildren, fall into that large and amorphous category of things-we-just-know, even as we can't quite remember anything else substantive about the subject. Perhaps we remember the date that the telegraph was sent (May 24, 1844) or its point of origin or destination (Washington, DC, to Baltimore), but little else. As with so many other things in this category of things-we-just-know, the notion that this biblical quote (it comes from Numbers 23:23) was the first message to be telegraphed is utterly untrue.

"What hath God wrought?" far from being the first telegraph ever sent, instead occupies the somewhat less illustrious position of being the first telegraph publicly sent through a commercial telegraph exchange from one city to another. The actual first message sent? It was not quite so heady. It was "A patient waiter is no loser," transmitted from one end of Morse's workroom to the other over three miles of wound wire. This platitudinous bit of semidoggerel was chosen by Vail's father, a judge who had been financing a good portion of the research behind the telegraph.[26]

The first few messages that were telegraphed as a public

demonstration of the new technology were hardly any more inspirational. On January 24, 1838, in a science classroom at New York University, Morse and Vail held a public demonstration for a group of scientists, telegraphing a message over a ten-mile length of wire. What phrase did they feel had sufficient gravitas to qualify as the first public words showing the glories of their creation?

"Attention, the Universe! By Kingdoms right wheel."*

And on January 11, 1838, there were reports that the telegraph had been used in Morristown, New Jersey, to transmit the rather prosaic message that a railroad car, bearing 345 passengers, had arrived.

On the one hand it is rather delightful to discover that so many of the early telegraph messages were either gibberish or mind-numbingly boring. I've never been that moved by "What hath God wrought?" myself. But at the same time it makes me question what other famous historical statements are completely different from what is commonly thought. It's as though I discovered that Neil Armstrong stepped onto the moon and said "Shave and a haircut—ten cents" rather than "That's one small step for man, one giant leap for mankind," or that Nathan Hale had gone to the gallows saying something flippant about the weather rather than "I only regret that I have but one life to lose for my country."

The telegraph is now largely a thing of the past, especially since Western Union, the one-time telegraph giant, stopped

* Some historians of telecommunications are of the opinion that this story is a fake.

sending such messages as of January 27, 2006. You can still send telegraphs in many other countries, such as Telegrams Canada.* For the most part, it is now considered to be either a strangely formal way to send a note or an amusingly retro one. Long gone are the glory days of the telegraph, when Western Union employed some fourteen thousand messenger boys to hand-deliver its messages.

Although it may now only live on as a historical anachronism, in its time the telegraph was a global phenomenon, one that made fortunes for many, shattered the way people thought about communication, and changed the world. It provided a far greater shift in how people communicate than email or instant messaging has. And yet it did not take very long at all for the telegraph to go from being a phenomenal invention to being a simple means by which two people could chitchat.

In a letter to the *New York Times* in 1894, Stephen Vail (the son of the inventor who worked with Morse) described a telegraphic exchange between the two great inventors two days after their historic "What hath God wrought?" transmission.[27,†] I am relieved to see that forty-eight hours after stunning the world with their monumental invention, Morse and Vail had already moved away from making any more grand pronouncements and

---

* Its website says, "You'll see why even after 160 years, telegrams never go out of style!" which is a statement that makes me wonder what other things this company is delusional about.

† No one ever seems to wonder what the answer was to this question Morse posed. Vail's response was "The city of Baltimore." Considering the current state of the city of Baltimore, I would consider this to be the greatest evidence I have yet seen indicating that if there is a god, he is an angry and vengeful one.

were chattering away over the wires about inconsequential and meaningless topics.

> **Morse:** Have you any news?
> **Vail:** No.
> **Morse:** Mr. Saxton's respects to you.
> **Vail:** My respects to him.
> **Morse:** What time have you?
> **Vail:** Nine o'clock twenty-eight minutes.
> **Morse:** What weather have you?
> **Vail:** Cloudy.
> **Morse:** Separate your words more.
> **Vail:** Oil your clockwork.
> **Morse:** I have a great crowd at my window.
> **Vail:** Oh! Ah!

Directory Assistance

Having established the means that people used to contact someone before there were telephones, let's look at what they did before there were telephone directories—how did they find other people? There was much less of a need to find other people in the days before there were airplanes, cars, or a reliable train system that could bring people to anywhere in the country they wanted to go. And although many people in the country may have had a vague notion that there were millions of other Americans out there, they did not have an overpowering yen to get in touch with them. Most people were far too busy working to spend much time wondering what the rest of the country was doing (farmers, who have very little time for leisure, made up 47.7 percent of the workforce in the 1870 census). For the most part, when people needed to find someone, they used city or town directories.

The first city directory that existed in America was printed well before America itself existed. In 1665 a directory for the city of New York provided 255 names of households, arranged by location rather than by name. It was a year after the British defeated the Dutch, under whose rule the city was known as New Amsterdam. The directory reflects the overwhelmingly Dutch heritage of the inhabitants of the city at that time. Occasional names from elsewhere in Europe, such as Guliam d'Honneur, are listed, but it is predominantly populated by the likes of Gertie Schoorsteenvegers, Peter Stuyvesant, and John Gerritsen Van Buytenhuysen.

This initial directory was the last one to appear in America for almost a hundred years, as no others existed until 1752, when a Baltimore newspaper printed a document with the curious title of *The Following List of Families, and Other Persons Residing in the Town of Baltimore, Was Taken in the Year 1752, By a Lady of Respectability*. Following this, an almanac in the South Carolina city of Charleston included directories in 1782 and 1785.

Later in 1785, Philadelphia became the first city to issue an actual directory not attached to another book or newspaper with the publication of two separate and competing books. The next year, New York issued its own directory once again, and soon after, all the other cities wanted to have their own.[28]

These early directories gave a good deal of useful information. The 1786 New York directory not only provided a list of many of the city inhabitants but also gave addresses and occupations. In the front of the book were instructions for where to find judges and lawyers, what the postage and exchange rate on coins were, the schedule of the mail, and more.

This first New York directory listed approximately 850 people and was only eighty-two pages long. By the early 1930s, when the city directory was coming to an end in New York, soon to be supplanted by the telephone book, it had grown to include over three million names and was split into three enormous volumes weighing twenty-five pounds in total.

In some cases, such as the 1850 directory for the city of San Francisco, the book had decidedly humble aims. This California city had only recently received an enormous influx of people who were coming to the west coast in search of gold; its rate of growth far exceeded what any normal city could accommodate. The preface to the directory makes this abundantly clear:

"It is not to be expected, in a City like this, where whole Streets are built up in a week and whole Squares swept away in an hour—where the floating population numbers thousands and a large portion of the fixed inhabitants live in tents and places that cannot be described with any accuracy, that a Directory can be got up with the correctness that they are in older and more established cities . . . we do claim to have done it to the best of our ability, under the circumstances, and leave it with the Public to decide upon its merits."[29]

This early San Francisco directory is 139 pages long and gives a bare minimum of information in most of the listings. The entire listing for city hall states "c. Pacific & Kearny" (which just means that it is located at the corner of those two streets).

Herman White is listed simply as "carpenter," with no additional information about where one might find him.

At the end of the list of names (the last one is for Andrew Zachresky, a lithographer), there is a good deal of other information that would have been potentially useful to someone who was visiting or living in the city. The entire city government is listed, all the way down to the assistant alderman, and included as well are the police officers, who numbered thirteen.

There are lists of where all the houses of worship were in the newly settled city and also where one could find diversion. Under the category "Amusements" is information on where to find the bullfighting ring, the Athenaeum Exhibition of Model Artists, and Rowe's Olympic Circus. The category "Places of Public Utility" lists two reading rooms, where miners could avail themselves of books to read, should they not care to visit the bullfights or the model artists.

For the entire nineteenth century, city directories provided all of the information that in the twentieth century people would get from telephone books—with the exception of the telephone numbers themselves. Often these directories functioned as a combination of yellow pages and white—they would list the names and occupations of much of the population and intersperse these listings with pages of advertisements for the retailers and merchants of the city.

For a number of decades, the two kinds of directories coexisted, until the telephone books made the city directories largely superfluous. Directories still exist, albeit in a greatly changed and diffuse form. There are directories of businesses, religions, cities, and even a directory of directories.

What's in a Number?

Telephone directories and city directories coexisted for a number of decades. City directories provided such information as occupation and address, and telephone directories for the most part contented themselves with giving telephone numbers (although some early versions listed occupations as well).

Since well before the actor Patrick McGoohan, portraying an existentially fraught captive in the 1960s British television series *The Prisoner*, proclaimed, "I am not a number! I am a free man!" people have debated the merits of attaching digits to individuals. Given that the telephone book is filled with both, it has seen a fair amount of this debate.

When telephone books were in their infancy, there was no need of numbers—all one had to do was give a name to an operator, who would then connect the call. Many of the first telephone books had no numbers at all. The rapid growth of the quantity of telephone subscribers soon made it clear that operators would no longer be able to remember the names and designations of all the subscribers in the exchange they worked in.

One of the first people in the late nineteenth century to recommend using numbers to indicate each and every subscriber was a physician in Massachusetts, Dr. Moses Greeley Parker. During an outbreak of measles in the city of Lowell, Dr. Parker worried about what would happen if more than one of the city's four operators succumbed to the disease. The telephone system would be paralyzed, since there were no surrogate operators who knew all the numbers and connections to replace them.

At first his suggestion was met with incredulity. Most people were of the opinion that subscribers would sooner give up their telephones entirely rather than submit themselves to the dehumanizing indignity of being identified by a number. Eventually, the obvious necessity of anyone being able to find all the subscribers in a telephone exchange won out, and numbers began to be used.

Compare the notion that numbers were thought to be so dehumanizing that people would not use them with the state of affairs a little more than a century later, in 1997, when it was announced that Manhattan was running out of numbers with a 212 prefix and that residents of that borough would soon be assigned telephone numbers with a 646 area code.

The city's public advocate office issued a dire warning that this could well have a negative effect on the real estate market, as people might not want to move if they thought they would not be able to retain their beloved 212 area code. Telephone companies such as MCI and Sprint argued that this gave an unfair advantage to Nynex, then the dominant telephone carrier in New York City, since that company would be able to offer more of these presumably elite prefixes.[30] Numerous individual customers worried that they might not be seen as "real" New Yorkers if they were missing the cachet that these three digits conferred.

In the years between, when numbers went from being seen as dehumanizing to being seen as a necessary accoutrement of living in New York, people have had a variety of feelings about them. For a brief period of time, telephone exchanges assigned numbers such that the first three numbers would spell the beginning of a word, based on the letter and number combinations that were attached to the dial. Soon after, this system was changed to use prefixes of two letters rather than three.

In 1961, when Bell announced that it would soon do away with the two-letter prefixes that started telephone numbers in favor of a protocol using all numbers, it soon found itself opposed by the newly incorporated Anti-Digit Dialing League (ADDL). The ADDL protested what it referred to as "creeping numeralism" and demanded that the letter prefixes be retained.

One of the founders of the ADDL was the prominent semanticist S. I. Hayakawa, who was quoted (apparently without irony) in *Time* magazine as saying, "These people are systematically trying to destroy the use of memory. They tell you to 'write it down,' not memorize it. Try writing a telephone number down in a dark booth while groping for a pencil, searching in an obsolete phone book and gasping for breath. And all this in the name of efficiency!"[31]

The first three numbers of telephone numbers beginning with 288 in New York were referred to as "BUtterfield 8." And once the 1960 movie with that name, starring Elizabeth Taylor, was released, people with that number had a far greater attachment to the prefix than they had previously. The telephone number for the Hotel Pennsylvania (Pennsylvania 6-5000) achieved immortality in popular culture after Glenn Miller recorded a song of that name that achieved great popularity.

Once people became attached to the letter designations, they felt a connection with the prefixes. The telephone company had not just assigned a random two letters to each number—the letters had to be able to spell the beginning of some possible word or name, and each prefix was individual to a particular area. The telephone company had unwittingly created a sense of community. It was based on numbers and semimeaningless words created by those numbers, but it was still a real feeling for the people with those associations.

However, no matter how irate the members of the ADDL and the people who gave up famous associations were, theirs was not the only viewpoint when it came to being known as a number. After the initial thought that people would sooner give up their telephone rather than be known as a number proved to be wrong, it became clear that some people liked their numbers very much. As the adoption of telephones grew almost exponentially in the early twentieth century, people were required to give up their old telephone numbers in favor of new ones with more digits. Many people were displeased by this and sought to hold on to their old number.

"Sixty Million Headaches Every Year"

One of the problems attached to the telephone directory in the early part of the twentieth century was the issue of how to get these increasingly bulky and heavy books to telephone subscribers. It would have been prohibitively expensive to mail tens of thousands, if not hundreds of thousands, of them to all of the subscribers, and so a variety of delivery methods were employed.

An article published in the *American Telephone Journal* in 1908 describes the process of hiring delivery boys and how the telephone company figured out how much to pay them. After some consideration, it was decided that they should receive one half cent for every book delivered, and in the early 1920s, one telephone company, in Muskogee, Oklahoma, hired a small army of local Boy Scouts to deliver the books via hand-pulled wagon. The Boy Scouts were paid both for books delivered and for books picked up.

The fact that the deliverymen were always told to collect these books (and if they couldn't, the telephone books generally had instructions saying to destroy or discard them when they were out of date) is why there are so few old telephone books left. I mean that in an entirely relative sense—I am sure that there are millions and millions of these old telephone books around, but compared to the number printed (which is well into the billions), there is a paucity of books from, for instance, the years 1944 or 1962.

The further fact that the books were constructed out of cheap paper did nothing to help their longevity. But plenty of other books constructed of cheap paper have lasted in greater quantities than the telephone book. The paper in telephone books does not simply disintegrate. The telephone companies have always stated that their goal in reclaiming old books is that they would like to avoid people holding on to outdated and useless information.

This is a difficult position to argue with. Telephone books are, like dictionaries, already out of date the moment they are printed, for just as it is certain that in the time it takes to produce a dictionary some of the words within have changed meaning, so, too, is it certain that in the time it takes to produce a telephone book some of the people listed in it have died, decided they no longer wish to have a telephone, or moved away and changed numbers.

Every year in the United States, millions of people die—from causes both natural and unnatural—meaning that at least some of their telephone numbers will no longer need to be listed, and approximately one out of every seven people move in this mobile country, which means there are tens of millions more who are changing telephone numbers.

After the first telephone book was printed in New Haven in February 1878, there was not much of a wait for the second one to be published—it appeared in San Francisco on June 1 of that same year. This telephone directory had 178 names of subscribers, and unlike its predecessor, it listed them all in alphabetical fashion.

Soon enough, one was published in New York City and another in Chicago; and all of the other cities where telephone companies were scrambling to institute telephone service were also scrambling to publish telephone directories.

A large amount of thought and research has gone into creating this book that children sit on to bring them up to the dinner table, this doorstop of municipal information, this thousand-page assembly of cheap wood pulp. It is far from being a slapdash compilation of everyone who lives in a given area, combined with their telephone numbers.

In 1916, a group of researchers led by J. W. Baird at Clark University in Massachusetts was hired by the New York Telephone Company to discover the most time-efficient organization of names and numbers in the telephone book. The researchers ran almost four thousand tests, in which they timed subjects while they looked up numbers laid out in various designs of the directory.

An article in the magazine *Popular Science Monthly* describes the experiment and states: "Care was taken that these individuals should represent radically different occupations and degrees of experience in the use of the directory."[32] The first part of that sentence is relatively clear—one imagines that they used bricklayers, physicists, and everything in between. But it is somewhat more difficult to understand what the varying degrees of experience in using the directory refers to, unless they meant that they used subjects both literate and illiterate.

The researchers stood by with stopwatches at the ready, timing their subjects as they labored to look up telephone numbers and then read them out loud, using books designed in a variety of formats—three or four columns to a page, indented or unindented text, and twelve lines of numbers per inch or eleven.

After thousands of trials, the team reached the conclusion that the best possible format was to have the listings arranged in staggered indentation, four columns per page, with eleven numbers to the inch. While this may not rank up there with such scientific discoveries as those of Galileo and Newton, it did enable the test subjects to reduce the average time it took to find a telephone number to 9.28 seconds, down from the previous average of 10.36 seconds with the older arrangement.[33]

The history of this book is replete with seemingly banal and inconsequential adjustments. This is in line with the development of many things in life that we take for granted, none of which began their lives fully formed, entering into our world

Athena-like in the shape that we know them now. The cars we drive today bear little resemblance to the "horseless carriages" that first intrigued and discomfited the population at the beginning of the twentieth century. This is due to the efforts of armies of engineers and carmakers, most of whom have made, at most, some small improvement to the design of the automobile, and some of whom have likely spent their entire career working on some small part of the car, in an attempt to make a small gasket even smaller.

The telephone book has no gaskets to speak of,* yet there has still been a great deal of tinkering under its hood over the years. Numerous editors in the past century have slaved and fretted over how much they could abbreviate the names and other information provided therein without making their book incomprehensible.

During the time between the 1930s and the 1960s, when the telephone book was growing enough to become extremely unwieldy, a number of measures were taken to shrink the size of the book. It was estimated in 1954 that taking out a single line of text in the Manhattan white pages was the equivalent of saving two entire books' worth of paper (each book was 1,836 pages).

A flurry of newspaper articles at this time detailed the steps the editors of the telephone book were taking to shorten its content. Not surprisingly, the titles of all of these articles tended toward the punny, with some examples being "Abbvtr,"

---

* WhitePages.com informs me that there are five Gaskets listed in the United States at the moment, but in my local telephone book, the Verizon White Pages for Manhattan, 2010, the listings jump from Gaskell to Gaskin.

"About—Tlphne Bk Abrvtns," "Edtr Tlphn Bk," and my personal favorite: "Mr. TMPLN Smashes WDS."

The TMPLN in question is actually Mr. Russell W. Templin, the directory supervisor of the New York Telephone Company for many years. Templin joined the telephone company in 1930 and rose through the ranks until he was supervising a team of a dozen other shorteners, all of whom spent their days inspecting the telephone book with but a single aim—to cut out all unnecessary letters and symbols. Prior to working for the telephone company, Templin had a short-lived career in the field of leather goods, but he came to the conclusion that leather would be ephemeral, whereas the telephone directory was destined to be eternal.

Templin was responsible for many of the boldest cuts that arose in the telephone directory, changing "lawyer" and "attorney" to "lwyr" and "atty," "precious stones" to "prec stns," and "ventilating" to "ventlag." Shortly after beginning his job pruning text, he did away with the abbreviation for street ("st") altogether and likewise banished the majority of periods, apostrophes, and commas.

The abbreviations themselves were sometimes abbreviated, as was the case with "residence," which used to appear after listings, in order to distinguish them from places of business. They were soon cut down to "res," which was then further shortened to "r." Eventually it was decided that there was no need for this designation at all, and the whole thing was abbreviated out of existence.

Every once in a great while an abbreviation would be undone

somewhat, although never lengthened back to its original state. When Templin had the idea of cutting "monsignor" to "mgr" he received numerous vexed queries from monsignors and managers alike and ended up changing it to the slightly longer, and presumably less confusing, "mnsr."

Templin was not the first to hold this position. His predecessor, one Mr. Brown, had held the position since 1918 and was the man who introduced the telephone dialer to such terms as "com mcht," "kntd fbrs," and "lds tlr" (all of which are Greek to me). But Templin appears to have approached his position with greater zeal than others before him, perhaps due to the fact that the telephone book he had to deal with was so much larger than the ones that came in the earlier part of the twentieth century.

So effective and ruthless was he at separating the textual wheat from the chaff that he once received an angry message from a business in the Midwest that was interested in using the Manhattan directory to create its mailing list. This company was convinced that the entire directory was written in some sort of code, and wanted to know where it could procure the translation key. Templin, not a man to take kindly to such deliberate misuse of his book, flat out refused to assist, saying that he had "no intention of aiding them in their nefarious schemes."

In 1954, the *Saturday Evening Post* ran an article on the telephone book, and some indication of the low regard that most people felt for the book may be found in the title of that article—"Sixty Million Headaches Every Year."[34]

The article is somewhat rare in that it is relatively long and about the telephone book, but it is considerably more rare in that it is about many of the small details of the telephone book that few would ever dwell upon, such as the fact that rats used to eat the glue that bound the books together (although mice didn't) until they added a substance that tasted even worse than glue normally does, which discouraged the rats.

The *Post* continues in this vein, informing its readers of the purported accuracy rate for the numbers in the telephone directories of 1954 (99.91 percent), the book's cost per volume to the telephone company ($1.50 for one of the larger books, such as those for Chicago, Philadelphia, or New York City), and the typeface used to print the listings (Bell Gothic, specially designed for the telephone companies and used in almost all telephone books of the day).

In addition to all the mundane information on how the telephone book was constructed, printed, and delivered, the article also makes mention of a certain amount of trivia, the sort of which is frequently mentioned in articles about telephone books. Readers learned exactly how many telephone books were shredded for a ticker-tape parade in honor of Gertrude Ederle after she swam the English Channel in 1926 (five thousand books). And they learned that in 1953, the directory for Cascade, Montana, still had a warning in it that obscene or profane language was forbidden to be used over the telephone wires, and that continued instances of such behavior would result in termination of service.

The readers of the *Saturday Evening Post* learned that there was a fellow in Altoona, Pennsylvania, who had the last name of Wolfeschlegelsteinhausenbergerdorff, which, at thirty-five letters, was the longest entry in the telephone book.* And they learned that in many cities across the country, there were concerted efforts on the part of some odd people to become either the very first or the very last name in the telephone book.

The desire to be first or last in the telephone book is not one I can readily identify with, never having felt its siren call. But it apparently means something to a rather large group of people, as this has been a common practice in enough telephone books that many telephone companies refuse to list names that have an unseemly number of Zs or As attached to them.

The policy on allowing names that are obviously fake has varied from place to place. In the New York directories of the 1950s, the last entry was held by William Kantor's Zyzzy Ztamp Ztudioz. The last entry in Los Angeles in the early 1950s was that of Ricardo Zzyzz (who was also listed under another, real, name elsewhere in the book). Yet many cities required that any subscriber who wished to be listed under such a name provide two forms of proof demonstrating that this appellation was used in other aspects of life aside from the telephone book.

Beginning in the mid-1960s, Bill Holland, a painting contractor in Los Angeles, decided it would be easier to tell people to look him up in the very back of the telephone book rather than to use business cards. So he changed his name to Zachary Zzzra, which put him smack at the end of the directory—that is, until Zelda Zzzwramp came along and took the final position away

---

* There is some debate as to whether Mr. Wolfeschlegelsteinhausenbergerdorff was born with this name, or if he picked it up along the way in order to enter himself in long-name contests.

from him. Displaying great tenacity, if not tremendous originality, Zzzra added several more Zs to his name and considered the matter closed—which it was until 1978, when he was once again made penultimate by some other rank interloper, Vladimir Zzzzzzabakov. Once again, Zachary winched a few more letters onto his last name and declared himself king of the Z aficionados.

3

OF CUTTLEFISH AND POETRY
Unusual Telephone Books

Most people, when they think about the materials that compose a telephone book (if they think about it at all, which is, I must admit, somewhat doubtful), think about the paper, glue, and ink that create the book itself, and perhaps some form of light cardboard that constitutes the cover. Few, if any, think about cuttlefish.

The humble cuttlefish (also called the ink-fish) is a cephalopod, related to the squid and the octopus and sharing their ability to change the color of their skin. It is an animal of interesting habits, particularly the male among some species, which is capable of such effective mimicry that the smaller members of that gender will shift shape and color to look like a female, so that they may sneak past a larger male who is guarding a female. These small and wily creatures will then mate with the female, while the cuckolded and larger cuttlefish zealously continues his watch for other males to guard against.*

Ranging in size from a single inch to almost three feet in length, cuttlefish are generally found in temperate coastal waters. Provided with three hearts and a donut-shaped brain, this cephalopod is strikingly beautiful, capable of shimmering its colors rapidly and producing myriad hues and tones.

Like the octopus, the cuttlefish defense consists mainly of squirting a thick cloud of ink into the water. Its main enemies are large aquatic animals (including other cuttlefish), although we should add humans to this category of foes. For in what would appear to be a rather poignant evolutionary misstep, the ink that was supposed to provide escape for the cuttlefish from ocean-bound predators was also one of the reasons it was hunted by humans. This ink has served a number of roles in book and photograph printing, and it has played a role in the construction of an extremely peculiar telephone book.

For several decades in San Francisco, there existed a telephone book unlike any other. The names, numbers, and addresses of the telephone subscribers in this book (between two and three thousand) were all painstakingly lettered by hand. The hand-lettered book was then given to a printer, who would use it as a template to make an engraving, which would then be used to print the several thousand copies needed for subscribers.

The reason these books went through such an unorthodox printing process is that they were written entirely in Chinese,

---

* Cuttlefish are certainly not the only maritime cross-dressers; male sponge lice also take on the appearance of the female of the species.

exclusively for the use of the Chinatown customers of the Pacific Bell Telephone Company in San Francisco.

At the end of the nineteenth and beginning of the twentieth centuries, San Francisco had the only foreign language telephone exchange operating in the United States. The Chinatown exchange was organized and run by a second-generation Chinese American, was staffed by Chinese American operators, and served a clientele who spoke Chinese; thus, it made perfect sense that its telephone book would be in the same language.

The Chinese American enclave in San Francisco is the oldest in the country, its roots dating from February 1849, when the ship the *Eagle* landed in its harbor. Its cargo was mainly tea and silk, but it also carried with it three immigrants from China: two men and a woman.

Within three years, this initial trio of Chinese immigrants, the first to arrive not just in San Francisco but in California as well, saw their numbers swell to well over twenty thousand across the state. Most of these new Californians were looking for the gold that was famously discovered in 1848 and so did not live in the city of San Francisco—they worked in the goldfields. After the first and most easily found caches of this precious metal had been found, the competition among miners heated up. In 1850, a law was passed requiring foreign miners to pay a fee of twenty dollars a month to continue prospecting for gold.[1]

Even though most of the Chinese immigrants lived and worked outside of San Francisco, enough others took up residence there, typically working as merchants or as brokers of laborers, to create a vibrant community.

The first telephone in Chinatown was located in a telephone

office on Bush Street. It was in use by the early 1880s, primarily by Chinese farmers who were selling produce or looking for laborers. Around 1890, a public telephone was put in the offices of *Mun Kee*, a Chinese language newspaper, and this was used by all the Chinese residents nearby.

A switchboard with thirty-seven telephones was installed in 1894, in a building at the corner of Washington and Grant avenues. These telephones were not connected to the rest of San Francisco until 1898, when they became part of the Pacific Telephone and Telegraph system, which served the rest of the city.

This exchange was run exclusively for the use of Chinese-speaking customers, and at the time it was the only telephone office in the world that was established for foreign speech in any country. The first manager was a man named Loo Kum Shu, who was a native Californian, born in that state in 1864.

Shu's grandfather had been one of the earliest immigrants to come in search of gold. His parents passed away when he was eight years old, leaving him to be raised in the home of a missionary, Florence Bokee. In addition to raising Shu, Bokee also helped provide him with an education, as she worked as a teacher at the Chinese Mission School. After graduating, Loo Kum Shu continued his education at the University of California.

By all accounts an affable and popular man, Loo Kum Shu served as the manager of the Chinatown exchange for twenty-eight years. During this time, he frequently gave tours of the offices, which had moved to 743 Washington Street and were notably different from those of any other telephone exchange in the country.

The Chinatown exchange was considerably more hospitable

than most telephone company offices were at the time. There was a functionary whose role was not to give tours (that responsibility lay with Shu) but simply to make visitors feel comfortable. The offices had a constant fresh supply of good-quality tea and varieties of tobacco available for any and all visitors. Loo Kum Shu lived at the exchange with several of his assistants, and through his stewardship, it became one of the most popular destinations to visit in the city of San Francisco.

The walls were covered with black lacquer, with gold and red trim. The switchboard where the operators sat had been finished with ebony, and above it hung a pair of carved wooden dragons. The entire ceiling was gilded with additional wood carving. Unfortunately, this fantastically decorative office was destroyed in the fire that ravaged so much of San Francisco in 1906. The new offices were built at the same site but were somewhat less ornate.

This new office lasted until 1949, when it was closed down and the numbers were integrated with the rest of the telephone system of the city. The prefix that this exchange was known by, CHina 5 (245), became YUkon 2 (982).

For many of the years that the Chinatown telephone book was produced, it was the result of the nimble fingers of a man named Sam Wong. Every year Wong would receive the list of the telephone numbers that he would need to compile into a book, a task that would occupy him for the next two weeks.

Since the lettering system in Chinese is ideographic (it represents ideas through pictures rather than through individual letters) it was not an option to have an alphabetized telephone book.

So Wong would arrange the names geographically, based on where in Chinatown each phone was located.

The calls at this time were all routed through the central Chinatown office, meaning that an operator would answer when a person wanted to make a call, and she would then connect the line. Even after the exchange had been in operation for a number of decades, many denizens of Chinatown refused to use the telephone book or to ask for a person by location or to give the telephone number for the party he or she wished to speak with—particularly members of the older generation, who often insisted on asking for people by name. Thus, the operators would spend a good portion of their first three weeks of training engaged in memorizing the telephone numbers (as well as the names and addresses) of the approximately twenty-five hundred subscribers. Even though they had a list of all the telephone subscribers at hand, the operators were still required to have a prodigious capacity for memory.

In addition to memorizing the names and numbers of the thousands of telephone subscribers, the operators were also familiar with the names of many of the Chinatown residents who did not own telephones. Thus, if someone called looking for one of these phone-free people, the operator could send a messenger boy to wherever the desired party worked, to alert him to the fact that he had a telephone call.

Many of the operators who worked in the Chinatown exchange were second- or third-generation telephone workers, as it was an occupation that a number of the original operators steered their children toward. These operators were required to be fluent not only in English but also in four or five of the dialects of the Chinese language.

Given that the Chinatown telephone exchange was so steeped in tradition, it is not at all surprising that in creating their telephone book they should have chosen to employ a man who would make it using time-honored methods.

In creating his list of the several thousand names that composed the clientele of the Chinatown exchange, Wong used largely traditional methods and materials. He drew the characters with a small brush, called a *put*. And in order to draw the letters, he would purchase a dried block of ink, called *mock*, made from the ink sacs of cuttlefish that had been caught in Monterey Bay. The mock was ground in a mortar and mixed with water. Once it had become ink, the remains of the cuttlefish were poured over a sponge, which would then serve as an inkwell of sorts, into which the brush could be dipped.

Cuttlefish ink was used for a variety of other things, most notably as the means to provide color for early photographs. These photos, which we often refer to as "sepia-toned," got both their coloration and their descriptive name from the cuttlefish, which has the Linnaean classification of *Sepia officianalis*.

If this telephone book were produced for an exchange in China, we would hardly bother to look at it at all. In fact, it seems likely that it would be regarded as some sort of evidence of a lack of technological progress, given that the letters and numbers are drawn by hand, using ink provided by a dead sea animal. But when taken out of context and moved thousands of miles from where we would expect to find a telephone book written entirely in Chinese, this specimen becomes a wondrous thing, unusual and worthy of being savored.

If, as is evident through this early example from San Francisco, the telephone book does not have to be alphabetized, in what other ways may it differ from the book that we are all so familiar with? In the early twentieth century, a number of companies eschewed the soon-to-be-traditional method of updating the telephone numbers of people who moved or who had recently gotten themselves a telephone—after all, it could be expensive to have to continually reprint all those books.

The New Ulm Rural Telephone Company in Minnesota was growing so rapidly in 1906 that it decided to do away with the fuss and bother of reprinting the telephone book (it would have had to print a new directory every week to keep up with the new customers). So the company decided instead simply to add the numbers of new customers to the local newspaper once a week; it instructed customers to clip out the week's numbers and paste them somewhere in their old telephone books.

This was not a method of updating the directory that had much success, as it was repeated only infrequently throughout the century.

Further Variations on a Theme

Telephone books, particularly white pages, have for the most part not embraced any great imaginative design. They have been the most utilitarian sorts of books, and most of the variation that occurs in them is the result of advertising rather than anything else. But there have been some exceptions.

One obvious variation among telephone books now is that they are not all printed in the same language. There is no official language in the United States, and although English is by far the language most commonly used, the 2000 census found that almost forty-seven million people speak some other language at home. The most common other language is Spanish, followed by Chinese, French, German, and Tagalog. Also included in the twenty most common languages, other than English, are Armenian, Urdu, and Gujarathi.[2]

Not all of these languages have their own telephone book, but a surprising number of them do. And in addition to linguistic variation, there are telephone directories (especially yellow pages) published for a wide variety of groups. There are Christian directories, for those people who want to give their business to others who presumably share their faith. There have been telephone books based on race, such as the Black Pages (also known as the Big Black Book)—a New York City directory geared toward African Americans.

Literary Aspirations

In 1905, the telephone exchange for the city of Pine Bluff, Arkansas, decided that it was spending too much money and time on updating the telephone book. It sought out a solution similar to the one that was unsuccessfully attempted by the telephone company of New Ulm, which printed its ongoing errata in the local newspaper.

Newspaper updates would not be good enough for the worthies of Pine Bluff. They had the idea that since telephone books and magazines both come out regularly with new material, why shouldn't they combine the two ideas into one printing? And so was born the short-lived telephonic literary digest known as *Everyone's Magazine*.

The Pine Bluff *Everyone's Magazine* should not be confused with the *Everyone's Magazine* published not long after in Yalta by Viktor Mirolyubov (a Russian opera singer and journalist), which contained such highbrow fare as stories by Anton Chekov. Nor should it be confused with *Everybody's Magazine*, an American periodical that published stories by, among other worthies, O. Henry. These other, similarly named publications existed at about the same time but had considerably more gravitas and fewer telephone numbers.

Published by the Pine Bluff Telephone Company, *Everyone's Magazine* was issued monthly. The beginning of the publication contained the listings of all the telephone numbers that had changed in the past month, along with advertisements.

After the business of fixing the new numbers was taken care of, the second portion of the magazine dealt with issues of local concern. Following these local articles were items more typically found in other monthly magazines.

One issue had a travel essay on New Zealand, complete with photographs. Short stories were published, although likely none by such as O. Henry. The back of the magazine was described by the *American Telephone Journal* as having several pages "of interest to ladies," meaning that it was concerned with articles on sewing and fashion.

"A Minute to Smile"

Sometimes you will find poetry that has snuck into the telephone book on its own, in fitful and almost random bursts, as in the titles of e. e. cummings poems that I've happened across in occasional yellow pages ("flotsam and jetsam," "Buffalo Bill's," "Little Tree"). Other times the poetry has been placed there intentionally, as is the case in the two small yellow pages published by Rodney Ryan in the 1990s and distributed in Long Island.

Ryan, who had the odd twin occupations of telephone book publisher and endocrinologist, said that he had hoped to allow people to experience some small amount of poetry in their everyday lives and, in order to do so, would insert small snippets of classic poems with the business listings, coupling the verses with such occupations as seemed appropriate. "When I go up through the mowing field," the opening line from Robert Frost's "A Late Walk," is placed near landscape contractors. With a mordant yet delicate touch, the line "Until the moss had reached our lips, and covered up our names," from one of Emily Dickinson's untitled poems, appears next to life insurance.

Each year Ryan spent an estimated thirty thousand dollars on adding the equivalent of fifteen pages of poetry to each of his books, and in return he received the remuneration that poets and lovers of poetry alike usually receive for their efforts—which is to say, nothing.

However, Columbia University did give a reading of his telephone books in 1995. The event, which was sponsored by the American Poetry and Literacy Project, featured Geraldine Ferraro, Joseph Brodsky, and others reading aloud from the poetic yellow pages published by Ryan.

Ferraro read her selection, Rudyard Kipling's poem "If" ("If you can keep your head when all about you / Are losing theirs and blaming it on you"), from the section on coin dealers. Ed Bradley read from the auto-parts section of the book, where Ryan had inserted portions of Paul Laurence Dunbar's poem "Life" ("A crust of bread and a corner to sleep in / A minute to smile and an hour to weep in").

Why don't we have more interesting writing in uninteresting places? The transit authority in New York has a program called Poetry in Motion, in which it replaces ads with bits and pieces of poetry in the subway cars. These snippets of poetry that I see on the rare occasions that I take the subway are by far the most enjoyable part of riding public transportation. And they are all the more lovely for the fact that they exist in such an unlovely place.

Having achieved the deep state of unhappiness that is commonly found on the subway, and being stuck in a stalled train with dozens of other people who have all achieved a similar state of unhappiness, might not seem to be the best time to reflect on poetry. But I can remember being in just such a situation, far underground, and having a smile involuntarily play across my face when I spied a poem by Kenneth Koch, "A Big Clown-Face-Shaped Cloud" ("You just went by / With no one to see you, practically. / You were in good shape, for a cloud").

What if the Internal Revenue Service had the wit and whimsy to send out a letter announcing an incipient audit with a snatch of William Butler Yeats immediately following the salutation of "Dear Taxpayer" (perhaps the opening line of "An Appointment"—"Being out of heart with government / I took a broken root to fling")? Would this not possibly ameliorate the resultant anguish for at least some small number of unfortunates?

I can program a machine to record the television shows I may wish to watch for all of the indefinable future. Online retailers can (and do) send me endless emails telling me what products they think I will want to purchase based on the clicking habits of me or my computer mouse. A movie rental firm recently awarded a large sum of money to several groups of researchers who produced an improved way of personalizing the ability to guess what movies people might want to rent. Why is it that we are able to personalize so many of the things in our lives, so much of which is of resounding superfluity, and yet we cannot personalize them in any meaningful way?

What if I could have it known to all and sundry who send me mail that I would be far more likely to inspect their epistolary wares if they happened to contain bits of writing from my favorite books? The rankest bits of junk mail would be eagerly opened and read. Even the dreaded sales catalogs, those unwieldy chunks of glossed paper advertising unnecessary goods, would merit a skimming if they included nothing more than marginalia from Bohumil Hrabal's *Too Loud a Solitude* ("For thirty-five years now I've been in wastepaper, and it's my love story").

I might actually read my bank statements if they began with a sentence or two by William Blake ("I seldom carry money in my pockets; they are generally full of paper"). While I can understand if the telephone company might resist sending me a bill that prefaces my monthly charges with the famous opening line of W. H. Auden's poem from "Twelve Songs" ("Stop all the clocks, cut off the telephone"), I would certainly admire it all the more if it did.

And once the telephone company had informed me of how much money I owed, it could sign off with a smile and a jig, quoting Ogden Nash in order to make me forget that I do not much care for either the telephone or the telephone company— "Someone invented the telephone, / And interrupted a nation's slumbers, / Ringing wrong, but similar numbers."

Form Follows Function

Whatever quirks and peccadilloes exist in our nation's telephone books, they have for the most part managed to avoid one particular one—they are rarely nonfunctional. For all their bland conformity, the endless rows of names, properly alphabetized and numbered, should come as a relief when one imagines the possibilities offered by telephone books in other countries.

An article in the *San Francisco Chronicle* in 1978 described the confusion that occurred when one attempted to use the telephone directory of Cairo, Egypt. The telephone company of that city was notoriously inept for a number of decades. One of the charming idiosyncrasies that doubtless became less charming as time went on was that the company arranged its telephone book alphabetically—by each subscriber's first name.

Thus, the 1977 Cairo telephone directory (which was issued in 1978) had listings for more than eighteen thousand Mohammeds—all in a row. There were 400 Mohammed Abus and 250 Mohammed Ibrahims. Each of these categories was further alphabetized based on the third and fourth names used by each of the Mohammeds.

This obviously made it fairly difficult to find a person unless you knew the full name and were willing to slog through a number of pages of similarly named people. One of the eighteen thousand Mohammeds in question was interviewed by the *Chronicle* for the story, and he was delighted to be so buried in the telephone book. He had accumulated a fair number of ex-wives and girlfriends whom he did not want to be able to find him, and this offered the perfect way for him to hide without seeming like he was trying to do so: "He thumbed through the 226 pages of Mohammeds until he came to his listing. 'See,' he cried, 'they will never find me.'"[3]

Judging a Book . . .

Most of the covers given to telephone books over the past hundred years lean heavily toward the bland. It is not hard to see why, as the books are not meant to be kept, and remaining inoffensive is considerably more important than provoking an audience's aesthetic sensibilities.

In 1985, the publishers of the telephone directory for Jackson Hole, Wyoming, discovered this when they decided to put a large photograph of what was assumed to be the attractive derriere of a cowgirl on the cover. Critics were not amused. Most directories, whether yellow or white pages, generally attempt to avoid such controversy.

These covers tend to be something most of us pay little attention to unless we come across one later in life, when it is a discarded or outdated telephone book, and find that the design, whether bland or not, tickles some long-held memory. The covers mean a good deal to the people who create the directories, and they run polls with focus groups to see what themes are preferred. The Yellow Pages Association of America has a yearly contest for the best theme cover, the winner of which is picked at its annual convention. The thematic covers that are picked tend to be those that are topical, as was the case in 1991, when the prize was awarded to a cover that depicted a veteran from the Iraq War reuniting with his family.

For much of the mid-twentieth century, most of the telephone books published in America bore an almost identical cover. They were illustrated with what was called "the Spirit of Communication"—a winged figure, clad in robes and clutching thunderbolts in one hand and telephone cables in the other, standing tall and proud.

This figure was a replication of a sculpture AT&T had commissioned in 1916 and which for more than sixty years adorned the top of its corporate headquarters in New York City. The sculpture, created by Evelyn Beatrice Longman, stood twenty-four feet tall and weighed about sixteen tons.[4] It now resides in the lobby of AT&T headquarters in Dallas, a city that was for many years home to another odd telephone book.

For more than a decade, the yellow pages in both Dallas and Houston were eagerly anticipated by thousands of telephone customers, although not due to any spectacular content within the book itself. The reason was the cover.

Every year for almost two decades, from the mid-1950s until the early 1970s, Karl Hoefle would provide a line drawing for the Southwestern Bell Telephone Company, for use on the cover of the yellow pages for these two cities. This was no simple sketch, however, but an extraordinarily detailed rendering of some portion of one of the Texan cities, one that would typically take Hoefle more than half the year to execute.

These covers are reminiscent of many of the illustrations that *Mad* magazine would have, if the illustrators of *Mad* had taken the time and leisure to spend upwards of six months in creating a single drawing, as Hoefle was wont to do. They are incredibly meticulous works of absurdity, filled with small bits of incongruity.

An oil truck, a fraction of an inch long on the page, has the words "Orange Juice" written on the side, undecipherable except with the aid of a magnifying glass. A clock on the side of a building has fifteen hours. Scattered throughout the city landscape are aliens, spacemen, and the occasional Loch Ness monster. Almost all of the visual puns, of which there are sometimes up to a hundred in a single drawing, require magnification to be seen.

On every one of the covers drawn by Hoefle there is a cat, or family of cats, always in some not-very-catlike place to be, such as crossing a busy highway. The cats were based on the illustrator's own pet feline, Pittens, who was in the habit of peering over Hoefle's shoulder while he sat at his drawing board.[5]

For a few years after Hoefle stopped drawing the covers, the artistic whimsy continued on these Texan telephone books, provided by another local artist named Norman Baxter. However, it is extremely rare to see any such imagination on a telephone book cover as these artists provided.

It would be a great relief to find more of these examples of whimsy and the absurd inserted into the accoutrements of everyday life. Whether they are snatches of poetry, silly and overly detailed drawings, or travel articles about New Zealand stuck next to the classified ads, these small chunks of incongruity have the power to liven up the dullest environment.

If the telephone book is destined to remain with us for years to come (and it seems at least possible that this is the case), it would be a minor joy if it were to emulate some of these odd telephone books of years gone by and infuse itself with some small portion of the unapologetically unnecessary.

4

LIVING BY THE BOOK

I f ever there was a man of whom it might be said that he was
bedeviled by the telephone book, it is Thomas E. Dewey—
onetime district attorney, thrice elected governor, and twice
failed presidential candidate.

Dewey took on organized crime as a specially appointed district attorney in New York City in the 1930s, convicted Lucky
Luciano on prostitution charges, was largely responsible for putting the notorious gang Murder Incorporated out of business, and
had Dutch Schultz planning his murder as a result (Schultz himself
was bumped off by gangsters who thought that murdering Dewey
would have a dampening effect on their criminal enterprises).

Dewey became governor of New York State when he was a
mere forty years old. He held this august position for three terms
and had a successful private practice as a lawyer after leaving office.
What trouble could the telephone book have possibly caused him?

In 1944, Dewey was the Republican candidate in the presidential election, facing the Democratic juggernaut Franklin Delano Roosevelt, who was campaigning for his fourth term. Dewey was the young governor of New York State at the time and facing an opponent who had greater name recognition than any other in the world. In the spring of 1944, *Life* magazine offered to run a large article on him in the governor's mansion in Albany, complete with a generous number of pictures.

The article, which is in the March 20 issue of that year, appears to be favorable to Dewey, making mention of his many political successes to date. He looks well-groomed and composed in almost all of the pictures, except for the one with the telephone books.

The telephone books aren't even in the picture, but they don't need to be. The last photo in the article is a shot of Dewey in the executive chamber, facing the camera. He looks oddly small, dwarfed by the furniture around him, and resembles nothing so much as a twelve-year-old boy who has put on a suit and painted a mustache above his lip. The caption below the picture explains that the desk and chair in this room are so large that Dewey needs to sit on not one but two telephone books when he has his picture taken there.

In reporting on this article, the *New Yorker* said "*Life* probably put an end to Governor Dewey's chances for the presidency the other week. . . . The picture of a postwar peace table, seating Churchill, Stalin, Chiang Kai-Shek, and little Tom Dewey on two telephone books, is plainly impossible. Goodbye, Pennsylvania Avenue; hello, New York."[1]

The fact that Roosevelt was six foot two and Dewey stood a mere five foot eight may not have had anything to do with the outcome (Dewey did manage a better showing against Roosevelt than any of the three previous Republican candidates who faced him in earlier elections—and they stood six foot two, five foot eleven, and five foot eleven and a half*). But looking at this picture and the attending caption describing the candidate's need to sit on two telephone books, one cannot help but think that here is another rebuttal to the adage that any publicity is good publicity.

Four years and change later, Dewey was once again betrayed by the telephone book in yet another presidential election, this time as he was facing Harry Truman, the successor to Roosevelt. The polls had consistently placed Dewey ahead of Truman throughout the election, right up until and during Election Day. The pollster Gallup claimed that Dewey was ahead 49.5 percent to 44.5 percent. Other pollsters said that the discrepancy was even greater, with Truman trailing by as much as 15 points on the eve of the election.[2] Few people thought the Democratic candidate stood a chance, including Truman himself, who went to bed at six thirty in the evening, after consuming a sandwich and a glass of buttermilk.

This evening prompted one of the most famous newspaper headlines ever, and certainly the most famous wrong headline, which appeared in the *Chicago Daily Tribune*'s early edition on

* Wendell Willkie, Alf Landon, and Herbert Hoover.

November 3, 1948—"Dewey Defeats Truman," it screamed in exceedingly large type.*

Of course, Truman won the election, not Dewey. And he won it quite handily, taking over two million more in the popular vote than Dewey and winning the electoral college by a margin of 303 to 189. There were a number of reasons why the pundits and everyone else guessed wrong in the election, and one of them was due to an overreliance on the telephone book.

In 1948 the telephone was not yet as ubiquitous a household fixture as it is today; it was more an implement owned by the upper class, the members of which greatly favored Dewey. The pollsters took what they thought to be the pulse of the electorate by calling random numbers taken from telephone books across the country. Except that they weren't truly random—as soon as they chose the telephone book, they unwittingly skewed their results in favor of the people who owned telephones and who happened to be more inclined to vote for Dewey. The good book is not as comprehensive or straightforward as it might seem.

Living History

The University of Miami has a copy of the last telephone book printed in prerevolutionary Cuba, before Fidel Castro came to

---

* I personally think that this was not quite so bad as the mistaken headlines that ran in both the *Christian Science Monitor* and the *Wall Street Journal* following the sinking of the *Titanic*, which read, respectively, "Passengers Safely Moved and Steamer Titanic Taken in Tow" and "Liner Titanic Struck by Berg but Passengers Are Saved."

power in 1959. The only one of its kind, it is kept in the University Cuban Heritage Center, along with over half a million other artifacts, books, and documents.

It is not so surprising that it should be the only one of its kind in the center—the papers and such have generally been supplied by Cubans who fled the revolution or defected in the years after, and who carries a telephone book with them when they are running from a war?

The book is one of the most popular attractions for visitors. While many of the visitors who come to see the telephone book are interested in viewing some form of the past that is personal to them, or to their family, there is another group of people for whom such a book is indispensable, and that is historians.

When much of the contact that one has with an entire country has been cut off, it is difficult to faithfully record and remember the minutiae of everyday life. The human capacity for such recollection is inherently imperfect. Some memories doubtless seem more important than others, or certain ones grow hazy and dim with the passage of time. Not so with the telephone book.

This Cuban telephone book has kept track of thousands of seemingly inconsequential details that decades later would be well-nigh impossible to reconstruct accurately. It is perhaps possible that someone would remember the address of the fruit store in a specific part of town, but there is no one who would remember the addresses of all the fruit stores in Cuba or how many of them there were in 1958. The telephone book has no opinion on the revolution or its aftermath. It strives, above all else, for simple utility and accuracy.

In 2006, British Telephone and the Internet genealogy firm Ancestry.com combined forces to put more than one hundred years of British telephone books into a massive, searchable database. It costs money to access, unfortunately enough, but is likely the largest such trove of familial and telephonic records found anywhere, with over 250 million names, culled from various areas in Britain during the years between 1880 (when the first British telephone book came out) and 1984 (when British Telephone was privatized).

What of the nonhistorians who use the telephone books for reasons other than to find a long-lost relative? What of the people who use the book for some purpose other than to find a telephone number that one needs to call? Well, there are people who memorize the telephone book.

Tricks of Memory

The operators in San Francisco's Chinatown exchange of yore were not the only ones who spent time memorizing telephone numbers, although they appear to be the only group to engage in this practice professionally. Lucille Noonan—another operator in San Francisco in the early twentieth century known for her memory of numbers—was reputed to have memorized more than two thousand of them. And Margaret Chase Smith, a Maine politician, worked as a telephone operator prior to serving as a U.S. senator for that state from 1949 until 1973. Smith managed to memorize the telephone directory in the Skowhegan branch of the Bell exchange where she worked.

The memorization of telephone directories is often described as an activity engaged in by people who are autistic, although it is not as common an activity for these people as is popularly supposed. The person on whom Dustin Hoffman's character in the 1988 film *Rain Man* was based, Kim Peek, did read telephone directories, and he kept a notebook with him while he did so that he could copy down numbers that he particularly enjoyed;[3] he also read atlases and many other kinds of reference books that purportedly discriminating readers eschew. Peek was able to recite from memory the names of highways connecting to thousands of American towns and cities, along with their ZIP codes, area codes, and television and radio stations.

Hedley Rice, less well known than Kim Peek, was a savant who was also in the habit of reading telephone directories; Charles LeBaron describes Rice in *Gentle Vengeance*, his memoir of his first year at Harvard Medical School. Rice was a developmentally disabled young man who would peruse the Manhattan white pages and, when visiting LeBaron in his office, would perch on the desk and regurgitate the numbers he had committed to memory.

But all these instances of phone book memorization pale in comparison to that of Jerry Lucas, the former basketball star turned memory expert.

Lucas was a member of the 1973 New York Knicks team that won the National Basketball Association championship. In 1996 he was voted one of the fifty greatest players in the NBA. Although indisputably an incredibly successful athlete, Lucas is arguably even more successful as a memorizer.

It is uncertain exactly how many telephone numbers Lucas memorized, as many of the accounts of his mnemonic prowess do not match one another. A recurrent claim (and one that Lucas himself never made) was that he had memorized the entire Manhattan telephone directory.

This tale, though often told, is highly unlikely for many reasons, not least of which is that, as Jonathan Eric Adler points out in his book *Belief's Own Ethics* (which is a philosophical examination of belief and doubt, and not a critical examination of former basketball players), it would have taken Lucas an entire year—8,333 hours—with no time to sleep or do anything else, if he could memorize an entire new seven-digit number every thirty seconds and not forget a single one over the entirety of that year (assuming, as Adler does, that there were one million names and numbers in the Manhattan telephone book).

The habit that some people have of attributing these astonishingly unrealistic powers of memory to Jerry Lucas is what Douglas Hofstadter, the author of *Gödel, Escher, Bach*, refers to as "a good example of how innumeracy can breed gullibility."[4]

Even with just a half-million names, this feat is well beyond human ability. So why is it that people so readily assume that Jerry Lucas mastered it? Probably because the amount of material he can in fact remember is beyond the comprehension of most people, so the number might as well be a million.

In the introduction to *The Memory Book*, which he cowrote with Harry Lorayne, Lucas estimates that he at one point had memorized the telephone numbers for the first column of the first several hundred pages of the Manhattan telephone book. Since the average column contains close to one hundred names, each one with a seven-digit number attached to it, Lucas is stating that he had memorized at least thirty thousand names and telephone numbers. Which would mean that, if true, he had memorized more than *two hundred thousand digits*.

Lucas would carry a telephone directory with him on plane

flights while the Knicks traveled across the country in order to have something to memorize. The journalist Tom Cheche described meeting with Lucas in a locker room after a basketball game—the athlete skimmed his eyes over a page of the telephone book and then handed the book to the journalist and told him to pick a name at random from that page. Cheche picked several names over the next few minutes, and Lucas was instantly able to recall the phone number for each one.[5] Several other people have apparently been partial to curling up in front of a fireplace with a cup of hot tea and a book full of telephone numbers that they wished to memorize. A memory expert in England by the name of Creighton Carvello memorized the telephone number of everyone with the last name of Smith in the Middlesbrough telephone book. I'm not certain how many Smiths live in Middlesbrough, or why Carvello decided to memorize the numbers for that particular name, but the city has almost 150,000 people in it, so it likely has a good number of Smiths (especially when considering that Carvello also managed to memorize the first 20,013 digits of pi, as well as the horse, jockey, and starting price of every Derby and Grand National winner since 1900—he wouldn't brag unless it was a large number).[6,*]

It is common enough these days to hear that people no longer need to remember telephone numbers, since so many of us own cellular phones with a built-in telephone book that stores all of our numbers for us. The Carvellos and Lucases of this world pay no

---

* Carvello held the world record for digits of pi memorized in 1980, but his record has since been eclipsed many times. The current world record holder in this odd field is a Chinese man named Chao Lu, who has memorized the first 67,890 digits.

attention to such pronouncements, as they memorize these numbers solely for the pleasure of having them bounce around in their heads, not because they would ever have the intention of calling all of the Smiths in Middlesbrough or all of the people in the first column of the initial several hundred pages of the Manhattan directory.

This kind of feat of memorization is never viewed as having any similarity to the attempts that people frequently make to memorize the Bible or any other such book. This is for the very simple reason that few people consider the telephone book to actually be a book.

A Book by Any Other Name

It is not only the literati who scoff at the notion of the telephone book existing as a book; the Supreme Court does as well. In a 1991 ruling that is still much debated, *Feist Publications v. Rural Telephone Service Company*, the court held that the information contained in a telephone directory was not subject to copyright and could be taken by anyone.

Feist had pilfered some four thousand listings from a directory published by Rural Telephone Service and was caught when the company unwittingly copied some of the fake listings that Rural had inserted for just that purpose.* Upon this discovery, Rural sued Feist for copyright infringement.

---

* These fake entries are sometimes referred to as Mountweazels, after the entry that the New Columbia Encyclopedia added for Lillian Virginia Mountweazel, a fictitious photographer, in order to catch those who copied the encyclopedia without attribution.

Feist lost this case at several different levels of the judicial system until it reached the Supreme Court. Sandra Day O'Connor wrote the majority opinion, and in it she stated that information and facts could not be copyrighted, although a collection of such things could be, if it had even the slightest trace of originality or creativity entailed in the creation of the collection.

Alas! The justices decided that the telephone book was entirely lacking any of this spark of creativity ("The end product is a garden-variety white pages directory, devoid of even the slightest trace of creativity"). The highest court in the land has decided that the telephone book, the book that millions of people refer to as "the book" (as in: "I'm in the book"), is in fact not a book at all.

I question this judgment of the Supreme Court—not based on legal grounds but on bookish ones. I have frequently heard other people accuse the telephone book of not being a book, and it is a charge that I consider to be absurd. Even when I point out that it is indeed a series of similarly shaped pieces of paper bound together, with writing on them, and between some sort of cover, they will still insist that it is not "really" a book and that no one ever reads it.

Often when mention is made of the telephone directory as a book, it is done in a gently scoffing fashion, some variation on the theme of "it has a great cast of characters, but I found the plot somewhat lacking."

But in addition to this cast of characters, which is frequently mentioned as the telephone book's sole redeeming literary feature, I would point out that it has at least one other saving grace—it does a far better job of adhering to the dicta laid out in Strunk and White's *Elements of Style* than do most books I know of.

"Choose a suitable design and hold to it." Although the telephone book has grown considerably since the first single-page directory was issued, one cannot say that it has strayed very far from its design, or that this design is anything but suitable.

"Omit needless words." I can think of few types of books, with the possible exception of certain atlases, that are better at omitting needless words than the telephone book is.

"Avoid a succession of loose sentences." No works of literature can hold a candle to the telephone book's adherence to the above rule of Messrs. Strunk and White.

While I will admit that the telephone book is somewhat lacking when it comes to following the dictum of "Write with nouns and verbs," it makes up for this in the spectacular fashion in which it follows the suggestions "Do not overwrite" and "Do not overstate." And probably no other book manages so successfully to emulate the following triumvirate of admonitions in *The Elements of Style*: "Do not affect a breezy manner," "Do not explain too much," and "Avoid fancy words."

5

THE PHONE BOOK HALL OF FAME

There is no object so quotidian or insignificant that it has never been grist for the mill of some collecting aficionado. For every J. P. Morgan (who managed to accrue three of the forty-eight extant copies of the Gutenberg Bible to round out his enormous collection of fine art and antiquities) there are likely dozens or even hundreds of people who collect used pencil erasers. It is easy to look down on such people or to erroneously equate them with hoarders, such as the famed Collier brothers, who filled an entire Harlem mansion with stacks of newspapers and unplayable pianos. But the avid collector of the odd ilk bears no more resemblance to your hoarding uncle (the one who keeps thousands of plastic cups in his attic) than a connoisseur of some simple fine food bears to an outright glutton. The things they collect may well be inexplicable to most, but that does not mean they are without some value.

In her book *In Flagrante Collecto*, Marilynn Gelfman Karp describes collections far more obscure than the tea cozies and bits of colored glass that we have largely come to view as the pursuits of harmless eccentrics. She writes of, and documents with photographs, collections of can openers in the shape of animals, butcher's display tags for cuts of meat, bride and groom cake toppers, an enormous category of the most unimportant possible bits of text ("shopping lists, Instant winner or not, do not disturb signs, keep this coupon, under penalty of law do not remove tags, sanitized for your protection bands, air sickness bags"), civil war propaganda envelopes, and many other things.

When it is tickling you as you try to fall asleep, a "do not remove under penalty of law" tag on a pillow or mattress is little more than a nuisance, and an unreasonable one at that. But when you view an assemblage of these tags, all neatly organized, culled from decades of minor law-breaking, and spanning numerous typefaces and styles, they assume a different character. A collection of mattress tags may be many things—it may be the thing that sparks memories in the mind of the person who collected them, anger in the person who did not collect them (but has to live with them), sadness in the person who simply does not understand why anyone would want these things—but each one is no longer a simple mattress tag. It is now part of a collection.

Given that there are such things as mattress tag collections in existence, it should come as no surprise to discover that there are people who collect telephone books.

Charles Eric Gordon

Charles Eric Gordon falls into that rare category of people who have a practical reason for collecting, as the success of his work depends largely on the strength of his collection. Gordon is a lawyer and private investigator who specializes in finding people, and very often he finds them through telephone books. I myself found Gordon through a Google search on "telephone book collector," although I didn't tell him this, as I was half afraid that he would look askance at so lazy a method of searching. When I spoke to him on the phone and told him that I was interested in coming to look at his collection of telephone books, he told me that he keeps them in four different locations, and that I should meet him at his offices in Manhattan.

Gordon is an affable man, wears a large ring with his initials on it, and offered me coffee as soon as I arrived at his office. Social pleasantries belied the vigor with which he'd taken on the far less socially normal topic of discussing telephone books.

As soon as I declined the coffee, Gordon began to interview me—"Where were you living in 1975?" he began. This was not difficult for me to remember, as it was the same residence that I grew up in and lived at for all of the 1970s and some of the following decade. I told him the street and building number, and he burrowed into his desk and came up with several large reverse telephone books from that period (these list people based on their location or telephone number rather than by name). Within two or three minutes he had discovered not only my childhood telephone number but also the names and telephone numbers, circa 1975, of everyone who was living in the old tenement build-ing that I grew up in. Some of them, like Mrs. Walters of the apartment above ours, I'd never forgotten. But there were oth-ers, like Mr. Roberts (who lived on the ground floor and used to accuse me and my brother of breaking into his apartment to steal his yogurt), whom I hadn't thought of in years.

The only error he made was not entirely his fault—he mistak-enly reasoned that my father's name was Brian, which it is not. My parents are of a somewhat Luddite and hermetic disposition and had only recently gotten their first telephone in the early 1970s. They didn't want people to be able to find them, so they registered the phone in my older brother's name. But it was still rather marvelous to see Gordon pull names from my childhood seemingly out of the air.

He explained to me that for considerations of space he had split his collection among four locations, and it was not difficult to see why. The office had enough shelves full of telephone books that the phrase "ten pounds of sugar in a five-pound bag" sprang into my mind as soon as I walked in. The desk was also entirely covered with telephone books, and precarious-looking stacks of them sat about the floor. The hallways outside his office were lined with enormous lateral filing cabinets filled with telephone books.

We each moved some small piles of books off of chairs and sat down while he told me how he came to become a telephone book collector. When he speaks, somehow almost everything becomes a referent for the old letter codes that were part of the telephone numbers of decades ago. He described reading tele-phone books as a child and visiting in his mind the places that the numbers corresponded to.

"Let's see, you had Coney Island, you had PR—President . . . that was where my grandparents lived . . . how much more dignified can you get than that? . . . President."

Indeed, almost all of our conversation was punctuated by the two-letter telephonic prefixes of a prior era. When I said that I grew up in the Yorkville section of Manhattan, Gordon paused the conversation and reminisced about what prefixes I might have had in my neighborhood (TRafalgar seemed to be his favorite). When he was telling a story about where he used to live or work in the city, he would inevitably mention what the prefix was for that area. But he mentioned these things so fluidly that it didn't seem odd at all that he was mapping the city by a series of coordinates that have been in disuse for fifty years or so.

Gordon freely admits that it was his childhood obsession with telephone books that led him to embrace them in his work as a private investigator. A lawyer himself, he works primarily for other lawyers, finding both those who do not want to be found (such as people illegally subletting their apartment) and those who might be happy to be found (such as people bequeathed money in the will of a long-lost acquaintance).

He is an inveterate searcher of information. When I asked him if he had ever come across a copy of *Everyone's Magazine*, that strange hybrid of telephone book and magazine published in Pine Bluff, Arkansas, in 1905, he cheerfully admitted that he hadn't but could probably find it. I told him it was not so important, but it was too late—his mind had already changed tracks, and he now had to find out about it. Gordon pulled out a handful of directories and manuals unfamiliar to me and spent the next ten minutes looking through them, still answering my subsequent questions but in a distracted and desultory fashion. He flipped through the books on his desk and consulted a few more, and soon he handed me a piece of paper on which he had written the telephone numbers for the five agencies or libraries in Arkansas that would be most likely to have a copy of this magazine. Having found something useful, he suddenly looked more relaxed.

Gordon hemmed a bit when I asked how many telephone books he owns, and it was unclear to me whether he had simply lost count or if he viewed the information as somehow proprietary. But he revealed that he's got at least a thousand, and none of them is small. Most of his collection is composed of New York City volumes, although he said rather dismissively that he also has some from Chicago ("But only a hundred or so").

When I asked him if either of his two daughters shares in his passion for the telephone books, he looked a bit pensive. "No," he said, "they think they're obsolete. . . . I mean, they know the prefixes, but that's it." He did not appear to think it at all unusual that his daughters would know the prefixes to telephone numbers they would never call, in neighborhoods they would never live in.

I wondered aloud if he had a favorite among the hundreds of telephone books in and near the room we were in, and Gordon seemed genuinely confused by the question, in a way that is possible only for someone who has an abiding passion for an entire class of thing rather than just a few examples of it.

He thought about it for a few minutes and then pulled out a Manhattan 1956–57 book, in a pale green color and adorned with a lovely picture of the New York Coliseum. I wondered for a moment if this was an arbitrary choice, the closest book at hand. Regardless, it still seemed fitting that he would have chosen a book that had on its cover a representation of architecture that was maligned as oversized and wasteful and was subsequently torn down.

Since meeting Gordon, I've often wondered about what class of collector to place him in. Is he a modern-day and unheralded J. P. Morgan, preserving treasures of the everyday for the future? Or does he fall closer to the camp of the collectors of used erasers and other people's shopping lists? I have decided that the distinction is moot. In my mind, collectors are defined not so much by their objects as by the associations they have with them.

In his book *To Have and to Hold*, Philipp Blom describes Francis Bacon as a collector of memories. It's a nice thought, the idea that someone would collect something as disembodied as memories, perhaps the least tangible and most valuable of all entities. After all, other collectors can hardly evince envy over your collection, and it cannot be shown ostentatiously or donated after you pass away—yet who would ever give up their favored memories?

I've come to realize that the telephone book collection of Charles Eric Gordon is composed of much more than the paper, ink, and glue—each book is imbued with the significance that he has chosen to give to it. Each book functions as a marker of sorts; each triggers a cascade of hopes, fears, and dreams of times gone by. Gordon's collection of cheap bindings and outdated phone numbers is no less a collection of sentiment than that which is found in anyone else's mind. The paper may be chipping and the covers frayed, but it is a garden of memories still.

Gwillim Law

Gwillim Law* is a collector of telephone books as well, although his motives are different from those of Charles Eric Gordon. He does not work with his books, nor does he seem to value them for providing him with a personalized sense of history. When I asked him why he has accumulated a collection of telephone books that exceeds one thousand volumes (and at one point had almost three and a half times as many), Law responded, "Why . . . all I can say is that it makes me feel good to think that I could find such a vast amount of information by knowing where to look."

He paused for a moment and then added, "And I enjoyed the view of all those books of similar format and covers lining up next to each other."

Law's telephone book collecting began in upstate New York, the state where he was born, in 1953. The Law brothers, Gwillim and Steven, began to collect local telephone books on a whim. They very soon became sucked into the morass that is the bane and delight of collectors the world over, the state in which collecting a type of thing does not require that it be useful in any way, only that it be somehow intriguing. Referring to a telephone directory he owned at this point, Gwillim wrote, "We began to see elements of beauty and utility in telephone books.

---

* For the benefit of those half-dozen people who will see a name like Gwillim and put this book down in order to go look it up to see where it comes from—it is the Welsh version of William.

Archimedes I Zzzyandottie was last in Manhattan but first in our hearts."[1]

An indication of how smitten with the telephone book the Law brothers were may be found in the fact that in 1961, while in sixth grade, Steven Law wrote a book report on the letter Q in the Manhattan white pages.

It is an utterly charming book report, all the more for the engaging precociousness that it displays; when asked for a summary of the story, Law wrote, "There is little I can say about this, for it is explained by the title. There are, of course, no events in this 'story.'"

In the portion of the report where he was asked to elucidate some of the things in the book that were worth mentioning, Law pointed out that the inclusion of the airline Qantas was of note, as "it disproves the q-u rule." Next he included a string of nine people named Quackenbush, due to the fact that "it shows that Quackenbush is a bit popular for a name," a sentiment that is hard to disagree with.[2,*]

Steven Law went on to point out some of the other aspects of the Manhattan telephone book that might be of interest to a casual reader, such as the fact that there were fourteen people named John Quinn ("this may seem strange to 'small-town' folk"), before summing up his experiences in reading about the

---

* Dr. Quackenbush was the name originally given to the character played by Groucho Marx in the 1937 film *A Day at the Races*. Before filming began, the producers thought to check to see if there were any actual Dr. Quackenbushes who might object. There were several dozen across the United States, many of whom said that they would be delighted to sue if Groucho so popularized their name. He was instead given the name Hugo Z. Hackenbush.

denizens of the Q pages ("The characters had no parts of any type, but they were used as well as possible"). I am very happy to report that his teacher responded quite enthusiastically to this project.

Steven and Gwillim continued to indulge in their passion for telephone books, finding new and inventive ways to add yet more numbers that they would never have occasion to call. Gwillim continued longer than Steven in this, and eventually he found himself with what is one of the largest collections of telephone books held in private hands in the world.

Gwillim and Steven badgered workers in a post office in Connecticut and were given a handful of volumes. Later they came across a telephone employee changing the books at a phone booth in JFK airport (back when it was still named Idlewild) and asked him for the old ones. The two brothers took a trip one summer around New England with their father and collected telephone books all along the way (for years they kept a large map of the United States, coloring in the areas they had managed to get directories from).

When Gwillim went away to college, he found a new and profitable means of collecting when he discovered that the library would regularly update six shelves of telephone books, throwing away the old ones. Telephone companies provided cast-off volumes, as did the long list of friends and relatives to whom the Laws sent letters to, asking for spare telephone books. The brothers made an attempt to place an advertisement with *Hobbies* magazine, so that they could find other collectors in their vein. Their advertisement was rejected by the magazine on the grounds that in Illinois (where *Hobbies* was published), the telephone book remained the property of the telephone company, and so collecting them would be skirting theft.

They tried to get other people interested in collecting telephone books, even going so far as to give away starter kits (which consisted of twenty telephone books, each one a duplicate from their own collection). These efforts were not usually successful, although they did clear up room on their bookshelves for new volumes.

After several of these attempts to entice others to join them in their unusual hobby, the Laws founded their own telephone book–collecting organization, titled OUTBAC (Organization of Universal Telephone Book Amalgamated Collectors). The organization existed for four years, from 1964 until 1967, and had a yearly journal (*JOUTBAC*) and a constitution that, tongue somewhat in cheek, laid out the rules and requirements of belonging to the organization ("I, _____, will neither steal a telephone book from a telephone booth, nor accept a telephone book which to my certain knowledge has been stolen from a telephone booth").

Steven eventually stopped collecting, and Gwillim slowed down his pace of acquisition once he was married and had children. However, Gwillim kept his collection intact and, until recently, continually maintained his website on the history of telephone books in general and his assortment of them in particular.

The Laws' collection suffered greatly after several disastrous floods and mildew episodes, the end result of which was that Gwillim was left with only about one thousand volumes out of several thousands of telephone books that the brothers had picked up over the years.

Several years ago, Gwillim began to sell off the remnants of his collection. His customers have included nostalgia hunters looking for a slice of their childhood, set designers looking for a period piece, and lawyers looking to prove that a particular business existed at a location at a certain time. He has also sold volumes to a few fellow collectors.

Law still has a website devoted to the telephone directory (www.oldtelephonebooks.com), although it has not been updated for some years. The site includes information on the many varieties of telephone books, pointing out that in various locations, the information contained in the front matter differs greatly. Hawaii, for instance, provides instructions for what to do in the event of a tsunami, whereas some of the San Francisco books detail how to respond to an earthquake.

The site offers some volumes for sale. The prices range from about fifteen dollars for fairly recent volumes (less than twenty years old) to several hundred dollars for those that appear to be rare (a 1932 edition from Hartford, Connecticut) or that would have some additional value (he has a few telephone books that list only the World Trade Center exchange from the 1970s; their pictorial covers, featuring these buildings, now look mournfully iconic).

Perhaps it is simply because I myself find old telephone books fascinating, but there is something ineffably delightful about the vast amount of information that Gwillim Law has posted on the Internet. He does sell these books, but there cannot be much profit in it. He has posted the Local Calling Area sections (those portions of the telephone book that describe the geography for a particular telephone exchange) for more than 120 telephone books from various areas in the 1960s and 1970s. Should you ever find yourself curious as to what the telephone number prefixes were in Fargo, North Dakota, in 1977, or Toledo, Ohio, in 1961, this is where you would go to look.

It is quite unlikely that this will ever be the case for you or anyone you know. But sooner or later someone who has wondered long and fruitlessly about just such a query will happen across Gwillim Law's website, replete with its photographs of books that no one reads anymore, and pdf files of numbers that no one else wants, and this strange and quixotic trove will make that person very happy indeed.

Madeline Schwartzman

Madeline Schwartzman is a filmmaker of experimental bent, a professor of architectural design, and an examiner of the telephone book. For the past fifteen years she has assigned the yellow pages to students enrolled in the Architectural Representation class she teaches at Barnard College in New York City.

When she first began using the yellow pages in the middle of the 1990s, it was mainly due to the fact that the book fulfilled certain criteria that lent themselves to an assignment for an architecture class—it was cheap, easy to find, and extremely laminated ("laminate," in design terminology, refers to the layers of an object, of which the telephone book obviously has many).

Initially, the students were simply required to make a path through the yellow pages by creating a series of voids, or empty spaces. It sounds reminiscent of the practice of creating a hiding place inside a book by cutting out a shape through a number of the pages in the middle of it, but the students were actually learning the difficult process of how to explore mass and lack of mass. Or as Schwartzman told me when we met: "One needs to be clever and patient to create interesting nonextruded voids in a mass made of planes."

For a number of years she would instruct her students in simply cutting away layers of the telephone book in order to create something new. But after the attacks of September 11, Schwartzman decided that she wanted the students to showcase some of the inherent character of the book and that future classes would need to incorporate some unique aspects of New York City into the project.

She considered the yellow pages to be the perfect vehicle to make her class interact with the city. It provided not only the right design materials but also the perfect content, allowing her students to explore the city through its ZIP codes, telephone numbers, area codes, voting districts, police precincts, businesses, and so on—and to explore the connections between them.

The halls outside of Schwartzman's office are lined with arresting displays of yellow pages. One has been chopped into confetti and then arranged into a pastiche of the island of Manhattan. Another has been cut to bits and attached to thin pieces of wood to create a structure that mirrors something advertised within the now-illegible text and slivers of paper. Yet another has further laminated the layers of the books and then turned them into some sort of staircase—beautiful and arresting, and signifying something I'm not sure I fully grasp.

I met with Schwartzman after she had finished teaching a class, and she was in a design studio that was half populated with students. She manages the rather neat trick of seeming simultaneously distracted and intelligent. Perhaps this is because she has the habit of keeping three conversational topics going at once, peppered with jargon and design concepts beyond my ken. There were copies of yellow pages scattered about the classroom, like the unused art supplies they had become. We sat down in her office as she pulled out copies of the work that her students of the past decade and a half had created.

The efforts ranged from the mundane to the spectacularly odd, but no matter which end of the spectrum they occupied, there was something magnificent—and slightly jarring—about seeing something as ordinary and familiar as the phone book transformed into one of a hundred newfangled creations.

One student had taken two books and created a scroll out of all the entries that fell under the letter *P* (which, for some unidentified reason, has the largest entry in the yellow pages). Another had spent the semester researching the type of yellow dye that was used to give the pages their distinctive hue.

Schwartzman's students have used the listings in the book to create an informative tapestry about numerous small ways that the city works—finding that there are no coffee shops of a certain brand in one kind of neighborhood, or stores of a certain culture or ethnicity in another. It has led other students to research literacy rates in the city, a means of finding out what percentage of the population could not read their own entry in this ubiquitous and brightly colored book.

The project I found most captivating was created by one of Schwartzman's former students, William Wetzel, who after finishing her class continued to look at the telephone book in fresh and surprising ways.

In one of his most memorable projects, Wetzel selected two numbers out of the yellow pages that appeared near each other but on opposite pages. These were numbers that shared certain geographical elements—they existed in the same city, they were in the same yellow pages, and they belonged to occupations alphabetically near each other—but otherwise had no known connection.

Wetzel then had the two phone numbers call each other at the same time, using a computer-generated dialing method, so that each party would believe he was the one who had been called. The calls were recorded and played back, so that this moment of serendipitous human connection could be observed and savored.

I am enchanted by this idea, as I am by most of the projects that Schwartzman's class has done. Reimagining the mundane is not an easy thing to do, and it is one of the most commonly overlooked antidotes to boredom. And so I can carry with me the notion that if the students in these classes can take a copy of the yellow pages and create something of interest and substance, then perhaps each of us can do the same in our own lives—make something new, using little more than some everyday materials, a fresh perspective, and imagination.

6

READING THE PHONE BOOK

William F. Buckley once wrote, "I should sooner live in a society governed by the first two thousand names in the Boston telephone directory than in a society governed by the two thousand faculty members of Harvard University." This is a fine thing to say, and it has proved to be an eminently quotable line (as well as showing off an admirable grasp of the subjunctive). Although I am certain that this famous graduate of Yale (class of 1950) truly did not want to be governed by the faculty of Harvard, I have my doubts as to whether Buckley actually had any idea who he might find among the first two thousand names of the Boston telephone directory.

I decided that it was high time that this book be consulted, if only to see posthumously whether Buckley's choice of government was the missing element necessary for a truly peaceful and just society. Buckley made this statement in 1963, and so I procured the most proximate version I could find, which was the 1961 Boston (and vicinity) telephone directory. The front cover has an assortment of monuments peculiar to that city. Some of them have the look of stuffy antiquity, and others are representations of proud and vulgar office buildings. The back cover is entirely composed of an advertisement for the Princess Phone, the telephone that AT&T began marketing in 1959 ("it's Little . . . it's Lovely . . . it Lights") as a more chic and expensive alternative to the heavy black desk phones that everyone used.

I made my way straight to the first two thousand family names. Here, laid out in logical straight columns, perfectly coiffed, was Buckley's solution for a well-governed society, ranging from a single Aaberg (Thomas) to hundreds and hundreds of Adamses (the last one being a Mrs. Winthrop C.).

Come to think of it, perhaps Buckley did indeed read through the beginnings of the Boston telephone book, and the extraordinary profusion of Adamses he found there, rather than the promise of government by the hoi polloi, was what convinced him that a society led by Bostonians would be preferable to one governed by Harvardians. After all, this 1961 directory not only includes such names as John Adams (namesake of the second president of the United States) but also includes those of his son John Quincy Adams (our sixth president) and his grandson Charles Francis Adams (U.S. congress member and ambassador to Great Britain). Maybe Buckley was so entranced by the idea of being governed by such a plethora of politicians named Adams that he overlooked the fact that all of these Adamses went to Harvard themselves and so presumably did not share his anticollegiate prejudices.

Indeed, there are so many Adamses in the first two thousand names of this telephone book (35 variations on John Adams alone, and about 580 Adamses in total) that a government as imagined by Buckley would resemble some sort of family picnic gone bad. We could have had a government in which every senator and member of the House of Representatives, as well as every member of the president's cabinet, had the same last name.

Cover to Cover?

After spending a few days reading through the beginning of this Boston telephone book and convincing myself that William F. Buckley never did get around to reading it, I set out to find anyone who actually had.

My discovery, which I think will surprise very few, is that there are not so many people who will admit to having read this particular work. When the phrase "read the telephone book" occurs in newspapers or is found online, it is usually meant in a figurative sense and refers to a particularly onerous or absurd activity. A typical example is when William Proxmire, U.S. senator from Wisconsin, described, in a 1982 interview, the speaking fees he had enjoyed as chairman of the Senate Banking Committee: "You don't have to speak at all. All you have to do is show up. You can read the phone book, and they'll be happy to pay your honoraria."[1,*]

Similarly, a fluffish article from July 4, 1965, in the *New York Times* asked a number of famous individuals of the day what sort of books they read "for pure enjoyment." Lady Bird Johnson was reading Hemingway's *A Moveable Feast* and Steinbeck's *Winter of Our Discontent*. Saul Bellow said that he derived his recent literary pleasure from Gogol's *Dead Souls* and Tolstoy's *Hadji Murat*. John Updike claimed that "fiction for me is burdened with a sense of duty," so he focused on reading small works of nonfiction, such as a treatise on the English badger and Sir Leonard Woolley's work on Sumerian excavations. Almost everyone quoted in the article claimed to be reading something rather Serious and Literary. Except for Peter Sellers, who claimed to be reading the *Encyclopædia Britannica* and the London telephone directory.

Putting aside the possibility that Sellers was having a laugh at the expense of the *Times* (a strong possibility), simply hearing his response does make one pause: why would anyone read the telephone book for pure enjoyment? The *Encyclopædia Britannica*, for all its absurd length and lack of a plot, is at least composed of sentences—and there is a plot of sorts within each entry, even if it is only concerned with the GNP of Finland or the complete works of William Makepeace Thackeray. Other people have been known to read this famous reference work or have

---

* Senator Proxmire may have lost his honoraria, but he managed to keep his royalties flowing, thanks to having published extensively in the somewhat thinly populated field of senatorial self-help, with titles such as *Your Joy Ride to Health* and *You Can Do It: Senator Proxmire's Exercise, Diet, and Relaxation Plan.*

dipped into it from time to time to browse extensively through its pages. But the phone book?

One might ask, Why not? There certainly are people who read other things that are just as free of plot, and they appear to enjoy this activity immensely. Facsimiles of both Sears, Roebuck and Montgomery Ward catalogs from the turn of the twentieth century have been published and continue to sell, even though they are equipped with no more literary suspense than a lunch menu, not to mention writing (especially in the Sears catalog) that may kindly be described as wooden. Yet people love to read them, even though (or perhaps especially because) they are describing a time more than a hundred years ago, well beyond anyone's memory.

In fact, the history of catalogs, unlike that of telephone books, has already been documented in trade books and dissertations. *Catalogues and Counters*—Boris Emmet and John E. Jeuck's exhaustive history of Sears, Roebuck and Co.—tells the story of Julius Rosenwald, the company president, traveling to Europe to visit bed-bound American soldiers. He brought with him several steamer trunks filled with the company's sales catalogs so that the soldiers might have something to remind them of home. The catalogs were apparently a great success in the infirmary.

Why was this so? There was likely nothing in the Sears, Roebuck catalog that these young men could have bought. And even if they could have managed to get these wares sent to Europe, it would have been of extremely limited utility to have a wheat thresher or sewing machine while convalescing in a hospital in France. But it is not hard to imagine the evocative power that the simple advertisements could have had for these homesick readers.

There are dedicated readers who devour other forms of

nonnarrative text. I have met a number of people who happily confess to afternoons spent poring over the Thomas Cook European train schedules—the older and more out-of-date, the better. Where once I thought these schedule readers madmen, I now think of them as readers with superior imaginations. They are planning trips to places they have never been or revisiting friends and places they once traveled to. With a small amount of practice, a travel schedule can fashion itself into the plotline for your very own trip from Paris to Tunisia in 1937, or any destination you prefer.

Elmore Leonard, the prolific and much-loved crime novelist, once imparted the following wisdom for aspiring writers: "Try to leave out the part that readers tend to skip."[2] In printing lists and prices of materials for sale, and lists of destinations and departure times, these publishers are leaving out all the parts that readers tend to skip—and then some. What is left is text so stripped down that the reader is forced to create a narrative himself. And if that reader has a substantially developed imagination, then anything may serve as grist for his or her reading mill.

Encyclopedias are filled with great concepts, and dictionaries replete with great words. Sales catalogs old and new are full of items that people want or are curious about. But these other kinds of reference works, these telephone books—what are they made of? They are made of memory and imagination. This map of gristle and bone is waiting for a reader to come along and add his or her own narrative.

In her collection of essays *Ex Libris: Confessions of a Common Reader*, Anne Fadiman states, "I have spent many a lonely night in small-town hotel rooms consoled by the Yellow Pages." Of course, this passage is in an essay she wrote about her fascination with reading sales catalogs, and it occurs shortly before she describes reading a car manual (twice). Fadiman is an utterly delightful writer, but she should not be considered anywhere near normal as far as her reading habits are concerned.

And so I looked elsewhere for mention of anyone who had engaged in this fruitless reading: I looked through card catalogs at libraries too antediluvian to have gotten rid of their paper files; I looked through a collection of books on American eccentrics that I've accumulated over the past few decades; I spent hours and days looking through the results spat back at me by various and sundry Internet search engines.

Having expired my libraries, I went further afield in search of someone aside from Peter Sellers or Anne Fadiman who had decided for any reason to read the telephone book. The first place I found that was reputed to have such creatures was the U.S. Senate, where the telephone book is apparently viewed if not as a great read then at least as a useful tool in filibustering. Filibustering is the old and much-contested practice, in the U.S. Senate, of speaking endlessly on some topic—any topic—as a means of delaying passage of a bill. It has the secondary happy result of so annoying your opponents that they eventually weep in frustration and acquiesce to your demands.

If this seems a rather petty and inefficient way of stopping legislation from passing, well, it is indeed petty, although sometimes it does in fact work. The trick appears to be to speak not simply for a long time but for an *interminably* long time. Hence the practice of reading from the telephone book: one imagines that it would take a very long time to read through.

Go looking for a story about the use or abuse of a telephone book on the Senate floor and you will soon come across the story of Strom Thurmond. This senator from North Carolina, who served in that legislative body for almost fifty years, was reputed to have read long portions of a telephone book during the twenty-four hours and eighteen minutes he spoke in an attempt to filibuster civil rights legislation in August 1957. (His speech still stands as the longest ever in the Senate.) I am no great fan of Thurmond, either his politics or his rhetorical style, but I was curious to see what telephone book he had decided to read. And one has to have some small amount of admiration for a man who has the fortitude to speak about anything for over twenty-four hours, even if he did come close to cheating by dehydrating himself in a steam bath before his talk, so that he could drink fluids without having to urinate. Plus, I'd heard that he also read aloud his grandmother's recipe for biscuits, and that sounded promising.

Well-nigh every speech made by members of Congress, no matter how hackneyed or useless, is transcribed and entered into the *Congressional Record*. This is now an exceptionally long work, and mercifully it is available online. I downloaded the entirety of Thurmond's speech, printed it out, and read it.

It is not something that I can recommend. And this is advice from a person who is keen on telephone books. According to listeners' accounts, Thurmond read his whole speech in a flat manner, devoid of affect or anything else that would somehow pique the interest of his listeners, and somehow the utter boringness of his mammoth talk translates quite well to paper—it is unspeakably dull. The *New York Times* described his readings of the Declaration of Independence and the Constitution thusly: "He read these monotonously, even listlessly, from the lectern, so that the classic phrases might have been so many items from the telephone directory." The paper also noted that, "Sympathizers, no less than his opponents, expressed dismay with the level of oratory rendered by the native of the Palmetto State."[3]

After trudging through the whole twenty-four-plus hours, I found no mention of the telephone book, or of Thurmond's grandmother's biscuits, but I did have the opportunity to become acquainted with the voting laws of all fifty states, since he read through them all. I suppose I should be grateful that Thurmond was the only senator who engaged in a filibuster attempt of the civil rights bill at this time. Robert Caro, in one of his biographies of Lyndon B. Johnson, reports that Thurmond's colleague from South Carolina, Olin Johnston, had planned to give a forty-hour speech but was persuaded not to do so by cooler heads in his party.

After the disappointment of finding neither telephone numbers nor biscuits in the transcription of Thurmond's filibuster, I became somewhat more skeptical about claims touted here and there that other senators had read the telephone book into the *Congressional Record*. Yet even so, when I found a rumor that Huey Long, the firebrand senator from Louisiana, had read the telephone book during his own fifteen-hour-long filibuster attempt in 1935, I couldn't help myself. I looked up the speech in the *Congressional Record* and read it in its entirety.

Long has always been one of my favorite politicians, and whatever moral and political failings he might have had (and they were considerable), they were at least somewhat ameliorated by a sense of humor.

In his filibustery way, Huey Long spoke of many things, none of them related in any way to the telephone book. However, he did provide fairly exact directions for three different recipes. The first two recipes, for fried oysters and for something called "pot-likker," were unappetizing enough that I would not care to inflict them on the imagination of anyone who reads this. However, the third recipe, for a Roquefort cheese salad dressing, deserves to be mentioned somewhere outside of the *Congressional Record*, and so I have decided to reprint it here, with some of Long's colloquial directions.

Huey Long's Roquefort Cheese Salad Dressing
(SERVES 3–4)

1 lb. Roquefort cheese

3 Tbsp. olive oil

2 Tbsp. vinegar

Approx. 1½ Tbsp. Worcestershire sauce

1 Tbsp. lemon juice

Paprika to taste

1 head lettuce

With a fork, mash the Roquefort until it is of a soluble consistency, with no unbroken pieces left. ("Do not take anything but a fork. Do not take a knife. Do not take a potato masher, or anything like that. That will not do the work.")

Add olive oil and mix well, for about five minutes, until the texture is fluffy and spongelike. ("It takes a lot of stirring. Any good cooking takes a lot of stirring and lots of mixing.")

Slowly add vinegar, stirring the entire time. ("You have to kind of gum it around a little bit, skim over it, until it catches up, and then mix it very slowly.")

Add Worcestershire sauce. ("You put in what appears to be necessary to make it fluffy and spongelike, and of a consistency that appears proper to the sensible discretion of one who is educated in the culinary art.")

Add lemon juice, stirring very fast ("so that it does not become clabber-like"), followed by paprika ("enough . . . to give it a fairly good red color").

Serve over one head chopped lettuce. ("It should be eaten with lettuce only. Roquefort cheese salad dressing should be eaten with head lettuce only.")

In addition to Huey Long and Strom Thurmond, Robert M. La Follette, a senator from Wisconsin from 1906 until 1925, is also rumored to have read the telephone book during a filibuster he engaged in during World War I. I have read through this filibuster as well, and although La Follette appears to do a fine job of annoying the other senators by calling for a quorum dozens of times, he does not read the telephone book at all. Not a single line.

So after spending far more time than is good for my health in reading the *Congressional Record*, I came to the conclusion that none of these three senators read any of the telephone book, at least not in their great filibusters (and I am using the word "great" in a purely quantitative sense). Yet the rumors persist, and I remain stubbornly convinced that I can find evidence of it.

Oddly enough, the only time it appears that the telephone book was actually read out loud as part of a filibuster was in 2005, when students at Princeton University did so in protest of the plan by then Senate Majority Leader Bill Frist to ban the use of the filibuster.[4] The students also read (among other things) the first several thousand digits of pi, so the choice of the telephone book likely had more to do with its length than with its emotional content.

One Reader's Quest

Well, why *doesn't* anyone read the telephone book? On the face of it, this question has a painfully obvious answer: because intentionally reading it would be the literary equivalent of engaging in pica, the eating disorder that causes people (usually pregnant women) to eat such things as mud and chalk. The telephone book is nonnutritive text: there is nothing there to read.

Or is there?

I decided that I would read the telephone book of my childhood, from the time and place at which I first began to use the book and first became somewhat aware of the world outside my immediate surroundings.

Energized, I set out to pick up an old telephone book and begin reading. But old telephone books are not so easy to find.

The New York Public Library has copies of the telephone book from every year, but it only provides them on microfilm. If there is one thing that sounds more potentially headache inducing than reading the telephone book it is attempting to read it on a screen, with the whirring clatter and asthmatic wheeze of the microfilm machine as background accompaniment. I demurred.

I looked around online for a copy of a Manhattan directory from the late 1970s, but they are in short supply, since few enough people are clamoring to buy these outdated and large books that booksellers reasonably do not keep them in stock.

My wife reminded me that Charles Eric Gordon owns some one thousand old directories, most of them from New York City, and suggested that he might have a copy I could borrow. I called Gordon the next day, and he was very eager to lend me a copy of the Manhattan white pages from 1979–80. When I went by his office to pick it up, he somehow convinced me that I should also take with me a copy of the yellow pages from the same year. I managed to escape without taking the foot-and-a-half-thick reverse directory that he suggested I look through as well.

The cover of the Manhattan 1979–80 telephone book is just as I remember it, or it is at least the same as what I think my memory of it is. Whether false memory or not, the cover looks familiar: a blotchy and faded painting of a downhill skier set against what looks to be a background of dirty snow, slaloming down a slope that is encrusted with blue and red flags. While this might seem an incongruous choice for an illustration on the cover of the Manhattan telephone book, it was chosen in honor of the 1980

Winter Olympics, held that year upstate from the city, in Lake Placid.

The painting was done by Bernie Fuchs, a one-time jazz trumpeter who turned to illustration after losing three of his fingers in an industrial accident. Fuchs painted presidential portraits with varying results (JFK loved his; LBJ did not), stamps for the U.S. Postal Service, and a large number of advertisements for car manufacturers over the decades since the 1950s. Eerily, Fuchs died less than a week before my little experiment in directory reading.

After looking over the cover, the first thing I do is open to my own family's name, to see the listing for the telephone number I grew up with. It is unclear why this is such a strong urge—I know the number, which has been unchanged for almost forty years now, and I've never had the need to look it up before. But the pull is irresistible, and so I look it up.

After reassuring myself by looking to make sure that my family name is exactly where it's been for all these years, I decide to start at the beginning and to read my way through, with no more excursions to names out of order.

But as soon as I open the book again, I fall prey to what for me is a distraction that is impossible to resist—I have to smell the book.

I have a habit of smelling books before I read them. Perhaps I should call it by some name other than habit, something that denotes a degree of pleasure. It is not a fetish, nor is it a proclivity, as I draw no illicit pleasure from it. I simply like to smell books before I read them. When presented with a new book (and I count as new any book that I've never held before), the first thing I do is open the pages to some random spot, insert my nose close to the binding, and take a good, hearty sniff.

If I am in a used bookstore and I come across two similar copies of a book that I want to buy, several criteria will influence my decision as to which I will purchase. I will be swayed by the condition of each book, by the design (if they are different editions), and by the price. But the smell of the book will influence me more than anything.

The smell of a book can tell you many things: how old the book is, what kind of paper was used to make it (high-quality cotton rag paper or paper that is glossy with a high clay content or flat and smooth and redolent of chemical), of what quality the book itself is. Sometimes the scent will tell a story of the individual book's history, revealing that the book has spent a long period of time moldering away in a basement, unread and unloved.

Occasionally I will look over the books in my bookshelf and reminisce over the ones that I've read previously and enjoyed. Sometimes I will just look over the spines and revisit the memories of what lies behind them. But other times I will take down a book and sniff inside. This provides an almost visceral memory of the text and the ideas contained within it, and it provokes memories that somehow feel more profound than if I were to rely on the visual cues alone.

My curiosity has been piqued enough about the influence of smell that I undertook to find out if there was any research that looked into the phenomenon. Happily, both social science and chemical science have examined the effect and influence of smell as it relates to both memory and books.

A delightful study published in the *Journal of Consumer*

Research in 2009 found that when scent was attached to an object, it greatly increased the number of memories a person then retained of that object and its attributes. The researchers discovered this by getting college students to come into the lab and look at pencils. One hundred fifty-one college students were given a pencil to examine; some of the pencils had been dosed with an aromatic oil, and some remained relatively odorless. The students were also given a list of ten characteristics the pencil they were examining was supposed to have.

Two weeks later, the students were asked to recall as many of these ten characteristics as they could. Those who had examined the scented pencils could remember, on average, 3.27 of these characteristics. Those who had examined the nonsmelly pencils could remember an average of 0.87 characteristics.[5]

I suppose we should be grateful that this knowledge is not something that was previously discovered and then applied in public schools as a possible educational tool. If dosing textbooks with a powerful odor was judged to be an aid to remembering the books' contents, imagine what olfactory trauma we would have experienced through our scholastic years. Perhaps if the book as an object survives long enough for olfactory science to identify what smells best allow the retention of certain kinds of knowledge, we will one day have algebra texts imbued with the essence of strawberry and economics books dosed with peppermint and a hint of motor oil.

For myself, I prefer that my books smell like *book*. I have long assumed that I am not alone in my enchantment with this odor, although I find that most people do not often speak of this. I have always assumed that the people who took note of this were a small group of enthusiasts, but recent research would appear to contradict that.

A paper published in the October 2009 issue of *Analytical Chemistry* (with the imposing title "Material Degradomics: On the Smell of Old Books") takes a look at the smell that is familiar "to every user of a traditional library." The authors of the study begin with rather poetic language, referring to the smell of old books as "a combination of grassy notes with a tang of acids and a hint of vanilla over an underlying mustiness." But soon after this they get down to brass tacks with a vengeance and describe the smell as the process that occurs as a result of the off-gassing of "several hundred identified volatile and semi-volatile organic compounds (VOCs)."

After a good deal of the sort of language you would expect to find in a journal by the name of *Analytical Chemistry* ("Lignin is a complex aromatic cross-linked 3D polymer"), the authors of the paper sum up their findings: old books have a special smell, and we know what it is.

There are many sorts of scents and perfumes you can purchase to enliven your olfactory experience of the world. You can buy an "air freshener" that will make your old car smell somewhat like a new car. There are sprays that smell like new sneakers, which I fervently hope are only sprayed on sneakers. There are sprays that replicate the smell of money or of innumerable fruits, and even one made by Burger King that smells like cooked meat— presumably for those unfortunate souls who live so far from a fast-food chain that they must do without the aroma of cooked putative beef.[6] There is even a company that makes a perfume that smells like old books.

Christopher Brosius is a perfume designer who makes what might be described as nontraditional scents. No cloying or simpering odors here; he has samples as disparate as Walking in the Air ("the Scent of New Fallen Snow"), Greenbriar 1968 ("a memory of my Grandfather . . . Pipe Tobacco and a healthy amount of Dirt"), and Mr. Hulot's Holiday ("breeze off the Mediterranean, driftwood, rocks covered with seaweed, and the smell of old leather suitcases"), named after the Jacques Tati film of 1953. He also has a scent titled In the Library.

In the Library's description calls it "English Novel taken from a Signed First Edition of one of my very favorite novels, Russian & Moroccan leather bindings, worn cloth and a hint of wood polish." On the one hand I am delighted that anyone would think to reproduce such a smell, but at the same time I am confused—why wouldn't you simply collect an assortment of old books and smell them whenever you like? I suppose it is far easier to have a perfume that smells old-bookish than it is to carry the old books around with you or to rub them enthusiastically enough on your body that the scent rubs off.

This particular book, the Manhattan telephone directory that was printed in 1979, smells a bit older than I would have imagined it would. It smells like a book from the 1950s, which may have been caused by its being locked away in a closed space for a long period of time or because it is composed of cheap paper. I cannot say that the smell of the pages reminds me of my childhood, since I was not in the habit of smelling books when I was six or seven, but it does indeed smell old.

I sit down with a fresh cup of coffee and an Art Tatum album playing piano encouragement to my reading. I have to confess that I cannot read the front matter. I find nothing of interest in reading about the long-distance rates for the telephone thirty years ago. I feel slightly chagrined at my reluctance to do more than glance at these pages. After all, someone somewhere sat down and gave some degree of thought to how these words about long-distance rates and the best way to cancel one's telephone service should be strung together. On the other hand, I reassure myself, someone once sat down and composed the text that is on the back of a peanut butter jar, and I feel no compunction about not reading that. I have a limited amount of time with this telephone book—Gordon needs it back within a few weeks to track down someone through its pages—so I decide instead to dive into the numbers.

The listings start with *A* . . . and then continue with *A* for quite a while. Nineteen different businesses or individuals have chosen to give themselves the name of *A* in the hopes of achieving an earlier listing in the telephone book. It is unclear to me how the decision was made as to which of these *A*s would go first. I can't help but wonder if the eighteen later *A*s were somehow jealous of the interloper in the very front of the book, and if they plotted his downfall.

Following the people who go by a single *A*, there is a small flurry of *AA*s (only three) and a pair of triple *A*s (the emergency road service and a locksmith). After this, a minor form of alphabetic pandemonium breaks loose.

The telephone company appears to have at some point become irritated with the constant attempts to move up on the line by having an increasing number of *A*s at the beginning of a listing and so has given up on keeping them in any kind of order. AAA

AAA AAA American Flag Dec. Co. wins the contest this year for the most superfluous *A*s, yet this firm is on page 32, the fifth page of listings. I had always thought that the telephone book had a strict sense of order and kept all of its names in rigidly alphabetic order, but this appears to not be the case.

Happily moving on, I see sixty-nine different firms that have chosen to begin their name with the adjective "accurate." Some of these descriptors make sense—for instance, we all expect, or hope, that clocks, watches, telephone answering services, and translations will be accurate. But it is slightly odd to see the other companies that thought that having "accurate" affixed to their title was a selling point, such as the folks who made the accurate flannel bags and the accurate lace dye. I do not know that I have ever come across a flannel bag that I felt was inaccurate in any way.

On page 31 I find another memory courtesy of the telephone book, although this is not one that I had hoped to find. I hit the listing for the A&P grocery store. This book lists seventeen branches, none of which have survived in New York. There is a listing for the store that was located at 1725 First Avenue, a half block from where I grew up. I have very few memories of the inside of the store, even though I was in it many times. Whatever dim memories I might have had of the aisles and of the food are obscured by the far more powerful memories I have of this store's garbage.

The A&P in question had a long exterior brick wall that extended down my block, and during the strike by New York City's sanitation department in the summer of 1975, it became the repository of the most spectacular stenches I have ever experienced. The sanitation department was on strike in the middle of a heat wave in July, and the citizens of New York were exposed to the quantity and quality of their garbage in a very direct fashion. My parents would carefully package all of our garbage in small plastic bags, which they would then place in the freezer overnight, as a valiant but futile attempt to stave off the incipient rot and stench that would begin as soon as it was placed outside.

Well over thirty years have passed, and A&P has not had a store in this city for many of them, yet seeing those two capital letters linked by an ampersand can bring back a memory of marvelous piquancy and disgust. It would perhaps have been preferable if the memories drawn forth by the telephone book were not of such effluvious horror, but that is the problem with alphabetizing your trip down memory lane.

There is no plotline to the telephone book, no denouement or catastrophe that will ruin my reading, so I can skip ahead to a memory of a smell that I remember more fondly, to wash out the stench of the A&P. I find it near the end of the book, under the entry for the Well-Bred Loaf. This was a bakery that operated in New York in my childhood and that baked its wares on the floor beneath the moving company where my mother worked. My brother and I would visit her at the third floor of the moving company warehouse, the entirety of which was redolent with the smell of freshly baked pastry.

The bakers would keep a stash of imperfect cookies on the side—those that had too many chips, or too few, or which were too large or small—and whenever my brother or I stopped by, they would give us one. These were cookies the size of two child's hands together. I realize as I remember them that I've not read any of the telephone book for a few minutes, and I am unconsciously puffing air through my nose with my mouth closed, in an effort, I suppose, to re-create the taste of pastry from decades past.

Visiting the Well-Bred Loaf through the pages of the telephone book has summarily banished the smell of rot that I found on the beginning pages with the A&P. I've once again decided against reading in order, and I skim the pages in search of other mementos of that year.

I happen across the Frugal Frog, a store that was located around the corner from where I grew up and one that my family would often shop at. The name did not in fact denote a penurious Frenchman but indicated that this was a consignment store of children's clothes. A bright green frog was painted on the outside of the store (in my memory), and the telephone book tells me that it was located at 1707 Second Avenue. I've not thought of this store in years. The simple act of seeing this name and address in print—not even a full line of text—triggers a thousand other thoughts and memories I likewise thought I'd forgotten.

Some nights I sit up late with my infant son, reading the telephone book. He is at this point just shy of three months old, far too young to understand what is read to him. I read to him nonetheless, reading things that I enjoy and that I hope he will one day likewise savor. I read him stories by Edward Gorey when he was just home from the hospital, and the macabre endings of *The Gashlycrumb Tinies* and *The Wuggly Ump* (all the children in these stories die horrible deaths) seem not to bother him in the slightest.

So I can think of no reason why I should not read him the telephone book. It represents some link to my own distant childhood, and some small part of me hopes that hearing the names and street addresses of these long-ago New York telephone locations will imbue him with a greater feeling for the city where we both were born. I know that this is an exercise in futility, but I know I will not be able to read him such utter nonsense for long, and so I am taking advantage of it while I can. For now, when I recite the names Abernathy, Abomelick, and Absalom to him in a silly voice, he is every bit as delighted as if I were saying something truly meaningful.

It is so enjoyable to browse through my own past through the use of this telephone book that I decide to compare the experience of browsing through this fragile and out-of-date directory on my lap with that of browsing through the online telephone directories that are now increasingly available. I search first for my own name. This admittedly is an unfair request to ask of the computer, since I do not actually have a telephone number in my name and have not for many years.

Nonetheless, I am offered a wide range of fifty-six possible numbers, none of which is mine but all of which belong to someone who shares my last name and the initial of my first. I have struck gold if I want to call dozens of other A. Sheas, but I do not want to do this at all.

To my surprise, some of these sites that I look at have information on me that I myself have forgotten, such as email addresses that I no longer use or telephone numbers in cities that I lived in many years ago. For a fee, I can access all of this information "and more," so they suggest. One of the sites that I am directed to through the Internet white pages assures me that it can tell me all about the online biography, interests, and blogs of this mysterious Ammon Shea fellow. And I am briefly tempted to purchase this portion of my own history. Yet it somehow feels tawdry to buy information, even on myself, and I resist this temptation.

The last name in the telephone book of my childhood is N. Zzherobrouskievskieskieea. An impressive collection of letters no matter if it is made up or has been mumbled down from one generation to the next. There is a long and rather sad tradition of people adding *A*s or *Z*s to their names in an apparent effort to be either the first or the last entry in the telephone book, although Mr. or Mrs. Zzherobrouskievskieskieea, I suspect, arrived at his or her spot the old-fashioned way: by being so named.

This practice of adding *A*s and *Z*s has been going on since almost the beginning of the telephone book, with a decidedly lukewarm reaction from the telephone company itself. The alphabet-wrenching name changers appear to be cognizant of the fact that they are somehow misbehaving—no one ever tries to add three hundred extra *A*s or *Z*s to their name; they just want to add enough to beat out the rest of the people in the list. Every so often the telephone company will declare "enough," and forbid its clients the right to emend their last names.

When I come across N. Zzherobrouskievskieskieea, I spend a few minutes wrapping my tongue around the name. Once I think I have a reasonable approximation of how N. would have pronounced it, I say it out loud to my son, who is eyeing me with the same quizzical gaze he wears so often, whether I am reading the telephone book or eating lunch. He betrays no surprise at such a name.

But I find the name surprising—it is not like most of the silly names that one comes across in the front or end of the telephone book. So I engage in what will soon be referred to as the time-honored way of sating curiosity in a half-baked fashion: I look it up on Google.

The name comes up a few times, more than I had thought it would. The first instance is part of an example for a definition of something called "variable-length field," a computer term. I then discover that although I have been reading the telephone book, which most people in their right mind would likely consider to be boredom unparalleled, I am not myself immune to being bored. Definitions of computer terms make me sleepy, and so I ignore this mention.

"Zzherobrouskievskieskieea" next appears in a link to what appears to be a study guide for Chinese high school students. The benefit of teaching high-schoolers using a thirty-year-old Manhattan telephone book is lost even on me.

The final hit on Google is for an article in *New York Magazine*, from 1979, titled "Hello, Central, Get Me Ronald Roach." Primarily dealing with names that were either odd or famous in the telephone book, the article was written by Ed Lucaire (who was also the author of *The Cat Lover's Book of Fascinating Facts*, *Celebrity Setbacks: 800 Stars Who Overcame the Odds*, and *Famous Names for Your Pampered Pet*).

The practice of a periodical running a story on the whimsy in the telephone book is almost as old and prevalent as the practice of adding *A*s or *Z*s to a name to change one's place in the directory. For many years, the *New York Times*, *Chicago Tribune*, and *New Yorker* (to name just a few) would reliably run a story on the new telephone book that had just been released. It seems to be a sign of the decline of the directory that such stories largely no longer exist. But when they did run, these stories typically had a minimum of content, instead making note of some of the silly names that were in the new book, how many pages it had, and perhaps how much the new volume weighed. Unimaginative and uninteresting in the extreme.

None of the writers ever look up their own name in these articles on the telephone book, to see if they have a namesake of whom they are unaware. No one ever looks up the name of their first love (or even an ex-girlfriend) or the name of the bully who tormented them in grammar school. In other words, almost no one ever treats the telephone book as though it were a simple book.

One notable exception to this inane approach to the subject is the *New Yorker*, which has always had a fascination with the telephone book, and the possibility of whimsy contained within, far exceeding that of other publications. Consider, for example, the unabashed enthusiasm demonstrated at the start of this article from 1937: "Probably everyone has his own particular little section of the telephone directory that he likes above all the rest. Our favorite passage is on page 983."[7] The piece goes on to celebrate the small passage of names from Twerdowsky to Twitty.

In 1964, the magazine ran a survey of all the Goldwaters in the Manhattan white pages, of which there were seventeen. Staffers called each of the people so named and asked them their opinion of Barry Goldwater, who was the Republican nominee for the presidency. Most of the seventeen were decidedly cool to the idea of their possibly distant cousin becoming president. "This whole Goldwater-for-President business is funny, but only in the sense that 'Dr. Strangelove' is funny," mused one of the Goldwaters.[8]

This article was such a success that a writer for the *New Yorker* repeated it six years later, calling all the Agnews (of which there were sixteen) in the Manhattan white pages to ask them their opinion on Nixon's then vice president. The reaction from the Agnews for their namesake was considerably more enthusiastic than that of the Goldwaters, although to be fair, it was several years before Agnew was charged with a variety of financial crimes and drummed from office.[9]

But such flights of whimsy are few; far more common is that an occasional newspaper or periodical will assign what appears to be a bored reporter to look through the most recent phone book and count the number of people named Smith or Johnson.

I'll not make the argument that this is a biblio-tragedy on par with, say, the destruction of more than ten thousand copies of the Talmud in thirteenth-century Paris, when the French crown decided that this religious work was insulting to Christianity and celebrated that decision with an enormous bonfire. Yet it is amazing nonetheless that so few of us take the time to rummage through the riches offered by these telephone books before they are destroyed.

I've just spent a few weeks roaming through these hallways of memory formed by lines and rows of numbers and addresses, and I don't understand how someone can look through a book such as this and not find something in addition to these purely factual items that make up these newspaper articles. Did not one of these writers ever find himself or herself gripped by a recollection that shook loose in skimming through the listings?

It is admittedly a contrived endeavor, this riffling through one's own memories by means of reading an alphabetized list of numbers. I could conceivably have found these memories by any one of a number of other means—looking through photographs of my childhood, reading the newspapers from the same time period, talking to my parents and family about what life was like back then—but how often do we engage in these behaviors?

Notably, the telephone book is as unemotional and impartial an observer of history as one could hope to find. Its judgment is unclouded by all of the vicissitudes that make human recollection of past events so fraught with inaccuracy. The order in which events and places lie within my memory is influenced by how important they were, or seemed to be. Some traumatic event or great success that occurred at some specific place will ensure that I will remember that place, and all the things associated with it, with far greater clarity (if not necessarily accuracy) than I will remember the name of the store that I walked by for most days of my childhood but never bothered to enter.

Yet these places that are half forgotten still form an integral body of memory. They are a backdrop, a chiaroscuro on the broader canvas of personal history no less evocative for having been relegated to the dustbin of my recollections.

Walking my fingers and mind through the New York of my childhood brings back far more than just the simple recognition of the fact that these people and places existed. It also brings back a well of sentiment that feels all the more vibrant and fresh due to its having been so long unexamined, as though these memories were a kind of newly discovered old stock that has been lying in the back storeroom of my brain for decades, still wrapped in its original packaging and never before used.

Inspired by this finger-walking through the book, I then spend an afternoon running past a number of the places where I would go after school. The Turn Verein was a gymnasium on Eighty-fourth Street, run by the benignly autocratic Mr. Schroeder. It had serious gym classes for aspiring athletes, and it also had not-so-serious gym classes for children like me—sixty or eighty of us would pack the small gymnasium after school to play dodgeball and inflict myriad other small cruelties upon each other.

Nearby was the Children's Aid Society, a public charity that was founded in 1853 by Charles Loring Brace either to rescue children from the slums of New York or to sell indentured and underaged workers to farmers in the Midwest, depending on whether you asked the farmer or the child. The Children's Aid Society ran a ramshackle and unappealing after-school program that I attended reluctantly. It also ran the Rhinelander Yard, the playground nonpareil for me and untold additional generations of neighborhood children—at least until the society decided to sell the building and the yard to a real estate developer.

Now examining this memory a little more closely, I can see that the Rhinelander Yard was actually just a mostly empty square of blacktop, with a handful of basketball hoops and some yellow lines painted haphazardly on the ground. But it still functioned as a playground for thousands of children, and I mourn its passing through these pages.

* * *

I can hear the voice of the sad-faced drunk who sat every day on his stoop on Eighty-ninth Street and called out a greeting as I passed by on my way home from school. I remember details of the occasional visits to Gimbels department store on Eighty-sixth Street with my grandmother when she came to visit—such as hiding inside the racks of clothes with my brother and the feel of the velour shirts that we asked her to buy for us.

I emerged from this journey refreshed with a new sense of my own past. I would not make the claim that this method will work for everyone, but I urge you to give it a try. Find an old phone book from some point in your life and take a trip through its pages and your past. Skim the pages or examine them closely. You needn't read it as one reads a book—the plotline is your own, and you can experience it however you prefer.

I did find one other person who had spent some considerable amount of time reading a telephone directory. In a letter written to the *Topeka Daily Capital* in the early 1920s, the dean of the Washburn University Journalism Department, Mr. A. T. Burch, held forth on the joys of such reading:

> I've just finished looking through a book with 16,000 heroes and heroines. Their lives are rather briefly sketched, but the sympathetic reader can guess that there is more romance and tragedy in them than was ever put upon a bookshelf.
>
> It is a reprint of many old editions. There are more characters in the new one than in any of the old ones, but some of the familiar names are missing. The passing of beloved actors

from the story has left heartaches, some of which will not have healed until the whole cast has been changed in future issues.

Then and Now

If reading the white pages amounts to a journey through the memory of my youth in New York City, then reading the yellow pages from 1979 amounts to a trip through the memory of the city itself. The city it describes is the same one I grew up in, but apparent in this book are the differences between it and the New York of today—differences so jarring that it might as well be thousands of miles, rather than merely thirty years, away. Yet there are also similarities, which oddly enough serve to make the reading experience all the more confounding.

Charles Eric Gordon had insisted that I take along a copy of the yellow pages to go with the white pages I borrowed from him. After just a few moments of glancing through this book, the Bell System Yellow Pages, 1979–80, it was clear that it represented a city so unfamiliar to me now that I decided I should read it at the same time as a recent copy of the same book, to see what fell out from its pages. Happily, Verizon drops a version of the yellow pages off on our doorstep with regularity. I have a current volume, garishly colored and even more garishly titled (I believe it's called superyellowpages, although it's hard to tell for certain, as there is so much text printed on the cover, advertising the worth of the book itself and its myriad advertisers), and I spent several evenings sitting between the two of them.

There is an immediate and obvious difference between the

Verizon yellow pages and its predecessor of thirty years: the recent one is written in two languages. One side is all in English, and then if one flips the book over, just like you could do with the lurid pulp mystery novels of the 1950s, there is an entirely new book waiting on the other side. In this case it's just a shortened version of the same book, but it happens to be written entirely in Spanish, which is not surprising, considering that the 2000 census determined that 27 percent of New York City is of Hispanic or Latino origin.

After establishing that there are obvious language differences between the two books, I thought to look at the two subjects that everyone likes to refer to as certain—death and taxes. In a charming burst of predictability, taxes are apparently just as certain in the various decades of the yellow pages as they are in real life. Both books list approximately 160 vendors under the heading "Tax Return Preparation."

Death, however, appears to be quite a bit less certain today than it was thirty years ago—the number of funeral directors and funeral parlors listed in the yellow pages has dropped from about 300 in 1979 to 120 today. I did, however, notice that there is an entirely new field advertised in the yellow pages of today— funeral preplanning, with twenty-three listings, where the older yellow pages had none.

Immediately after "Funerals" comes "Fur," which, it turns out, was also considerably more popular thirty years ago than it is today. The Verizon superyellowpages has but a single page of listings for fur, divided among the following aspects of the fur trade: retail, storage, buyers, consultants, designers, dyers, matching, renting, and novelties and accessories.

The yellow pages of 1979 bespeaks a much greater attachment

to the fur trade (on the consumer's behalf, if not the animals'). There are more than eight pages of listings, detailing hundreds and hundreds of dealers in pelts of all kinds. So voluminous are the choices that there is even included a guide at the beginning of this section, describing who sells what kind of fur. So in the event that you were curious about who was selling opossum fur in New York in the 1970s (Moe Lippman and Harry Kirshner), now you know.

Even just by browsing through the older yellow pages one can see the myriad ways that the commercial world of New York has changed. We are no longer a city that produces goods, and this is reflected by the fact that the sixteen-and-a-half-page section of "Exporters" has dwindled away entirely to nothing.

In some cases the differences in listings between these two books may be representative of the changes in industry in New York, or it may simply be that the newer yellow pages has dispensed with listing some of the smaller categories of merchant (in a single small section of the old yellow pages one can find all the stores that deal in spangles, spectacle cases, or sponges). There is a far greater number of types of merchants and tradesmen listed as well—in 1979 if one had need of someone to repaint a smokestack (a predicament common to us all), one could find a variety of people suited to this task under the section exclusively devoted to "smokestack painting."

A handful of establishments in New York still deal with typewriters, either to sell or to repair them, but it seems obvious that they know they are in a declining field. There is but a single store that has chosen to run an ad in the small corner of the current telephone directory that deals with typewriters. It reads, "YES! We still repair IBM Selectric and Wheelwriter Typewriters"— with an enthusiasm that feels born of desperation.

Looking to the yellow pages of 1979, one can immediately see that the typewriter was, if not king, at least a very important duke. The book has more than a dozen pages of ads and listings, and the typewriter companies spent their money freely, taking half-page ads. Rather than the plaintive tone adopted in the single ad found in the current yellow pages, these ads have a tone of exclusivity and sound drunk on their own allure, whispering such silken blandishments as "For people who take their words seriously."

Other forms of societal change are evident as well. The change (read: decline) in our reading habits has been documented in a paper the National Endowment for the Arts released in 2003. It found that we are reading less. I am sure the researchers employed a fine methodology in discovering this, but one could also have compared the yellow pages of New York today (which has approximately two pages of listings for bookstores, both new and used) with an edition from thirty years past (which boasts seven and a half pages of such listings) and come to the same conclusion, albeit less scientifically.

However, not all of the changes viewable in the yellow pages are indicative of a moral or intellectual decline. The only listings that deal with asbestos in today's book are for the removal of it or to have it inspected or tested. In 1979, one could buy, in the words of an advertiser, "all types of asbestos materials and insulations." There were asbestos suppliers, asbestos contractors, asbestos pipe coverers, and even asbestos siding. I find that I am mildly surprised that there are no advertisements for asbestos lollipops or asbestos-lined children's garments.

You can read of the shift that technology has wrought in our lives in these yellow pages. The older book has more than twenty pages of ads and listings for telephone answering services, a section that does not exist at all in today's directory. Inexorable progress has rendered this occupation obsolete.

There is no "Computer" heading in the 1979 yellow pages. Although computers were sold at the time, they were all to be found in the section marked "Computing Devices," which took up a single column. However, one could still find a number of establishments that would engross* a scroll for you. And if you needed coal, coal brokers, coal miners, or coal stokers, these things could all be found in 1979.

The newer book has more information in the front than the older one does. It has maps of many of the parks in the city, guides to nightlife and restaurants, a list of telephone numbers that it describes, oddly, as "hard to find," and more bells and whistles than I can count.

Though it should be noted that the current book lists neither "Bells" nor "Whistles" among its categories, skipping straight from "Beer Homebrewing Equip. & Supplies" to "Belts and Suspenders" and from "Whirlpool Bath Equip. & Supplies" to "Wigs & Hair Pieces," the older book *does* have listings for both bells ("Verdin Church Bells And Carillions") and whistles ("Buglecraft Inc.—Official Police & Military Whistles").

The number of listings in the yellow pages has changed over

---

* This somewhat archaic meaning of "engross," which was the word's original one in English, is defined in the *Oxford English Dictionary* as "To write in large letters; chiefly, and now almost exclusively, to write in a peculiar character appropriate to legal documents; *hence*, to write out or express in legal form."

the past few decades, with the trend leaning toward having fewer listings overall. This may in general lead to nothing more than less specificity, but on occasion it can cause greater hardship than simply not finding someone to paint your smokestack.

After all, this is not information that you can easily find through Google or any other online search engine. True, knowing who was selling opossum fur in New York thirty years ago is not likely to be at the top of many people's things-I-need-to-know list, but why is it that we should only choose to preserve the information that a plurality of people want to know?

Time and time again I have gone to libraries in search of some old telephone book, only to be told that the book in question has not been preserved. Typically the staff person adopts a slightly apologetic tone in delivering this news, along with some sort of muttered explanation, such as "Not too many people are interested in that sort of thing" or "We don't get too many people who are interested in old telephone books."

But what will happen if we as a people decide to focus our energies on retaining the sorts of things that most people are interested in? What sorts of things *are* people interested in?

One day, after yet another librarian informed me that the collection had no old copies of telephone directories due to the fact that not many people were interested in these things, I sat down at my computer and began to look for what it is that people are looking for knowledge on.

When I looked at Ask.com, one of the popular search engines online, it informed me that the most commonly looked-for subjects in the past week were "Facebook," "YouTube," and the generic subject of "flowers." These are not indicative of a tremendous intellectual curiosity. But this is the Christmas season, and perhaps I am unfairly judging the computer-using public; maybe as a people we are all overfull of forced holiday cheer and unable to interest ourselves in things any deeper than social networking sites and floral arrangements. What things are we interested in, as indicated by computer searches, in a broader time period?

The Internet site Lycos informs me that in 2008, the most recent year for which it has the information available, the most searched-for items were "poker," "Paris Hilton," and "YouTube." This represents an enormous shift from the previous year, when the three most searched-for items were "poker," "MySpace," and "Britney Spears." In 2006 the top three were "poker," "MySpace," and "RuneScape" (an online adventure game that narrowly beat out "Pamela Anderson" for the bronze medal of vacuity).

So if we, and our libraries, are to plan accordingly and keep at hand only such things as the general public is interested in, then, by all means, we should throw away all of the old telephone books and begin stockpiling materials that relate to gambling, social networking, and young women of ephemeral celebrity.

Where Have All the Phone Books Gone?

The New York Public Library, an institution in which I have spent an enormous portion of my life happily burrowing about, is one of the greatest repositories of information (both useful and useless) in the world. It has millions of items and generally does a fine job of making them available to the public.

In fact, the New York Public Library once had a great history of keeping what might be thought of as unnecessary telephone books. During World War II, the Forty-second Street branch had a collection of telephone books from all over the world, which was much in demand among army intelligence officers. The armed services would periodically send over an artillery commander, who would sit there poring over telephone books of far-off lands, comparing numbers with maps in order to pick and place targets.

Yet such methods of waging war are long since gone, the artillery commanders have stopped coming by, and the New York Public Library (NYPL), as fine an institution as it is, is not immune to the practice of making things inaccessible because most people are not interested in them. This is an inescapable necessity; libraries, even those as large as the NYPL, just do not have enough room to keep all of their materials close at hand.

On the one hand, putting books that are infrequently read in storage would seem to be a logical solution to the problem of limited space. As long as the books can eventually be found, there is no real loss to the person who wants to read them—one just has to wait a day or two before they can be retrieved.

And yet something very real is lost by this system, and that is the joy of browsing, the benefits of which are both tangible and intangible and are often overlooked. Anyone who frequents libraries or bookstores is familiar with the frisson of excitement that comes from discovering a desirable book that has never been read or, even better, an entire shelf of them, laden with dust and promise. This is an excitement that cannot quite be replicated by reading a computer screen that has a list of books that have never been read and that are being held in a storage facility in the next state, but which can be made available to you in a few days, provided you fill out some call slips.

Browsing, whether it is through a bookstore, a library, or a book, is not the same as reading a book with the express purpose of finding something concrete. It is an almost abstract form of reading, without any of the confines of plot, pagination, or the expectation of specific results.

Thoughts are often triggered by something unexpected. A fact falls out of a paragraph or off of the dust jacket of a book, catches my eye, and causes me to scurry further down the shelf or through the pages, looking for something related that may or may not be there. I can easily spend an hour or two looking through the indices, bibliographies, or acknowledgments in a shelf of books. These are treasure maps for the browser, and the pure joy that comes from discovering an unknown unknown* in this nonnarrative text is utterly lost when I have to wait two days to look at a book.

Some while ago, I went to the main research branch of the NYPL in search of the 1963 Boston telephone book, so that I could look at those first two thousand names that William F. Buckley held up as a preferable source of good government. Its records indicated that the library had this volume on microfilm, which is no way to read a book, but I reasoned that I could at least print a paper copy of the names and pretend that I was reading a book.

The microfilm was no longer there, and a clerk informed me that the library had "lent" several hundred phone books on

---

* This is the only time in this book that I will quote or paraphrase Donald Rumsfeld.

film to the Library of Congress twenty years earlier and did not know when they would be returned. A reference librarian found a paper copy of this book that was being kept in an off-site storage facility, and so I filled out a slip and waited for a week.

I had been given a telephone number to call to check on the arrival of this book, and so when the appointed day came, I dialed the number (with, I must confess, a small excitement, although nothing like I would have felt had I come across the book on a shelf). The disembodied voice I spoke with spent some time rummaging about looking for my book and then informed me that it had been lost at some point in the past few years, and the tone of the man's voice indicated that he had neither the expectation of finding it nor the inclination.

After the libraries failed me in my attempt to locate a copy of the Boston telephone book from the early 1960s, I turned to the new library—the web. At my wife's urging, and with great skepticism on my part, I placed an ad at Craigslist in Boston, explaining that I was looking for a copy of the Boston white pages from 1963. I posted the ad at ten in the evening, and when I woke the next morning, I found that I had received a reply from a Bostonian who offered me photocopies of his 1961 white pages.

The owner of this outdated list of telephone numbers, one Henry Dane, had purchased it at an estate sale some years back, as he had grown up in the area and it had some of his family's listings in it. He said he was drawn to it because he writes fiction that is set in that area and time and thought the book would provide interesting reference points.

When Henry wrote, he said that he wasn't interested in selling his telephone book but would be happy to look up some numbers for me, if that was what I needed. I responded that I didn't want the whole book, just the first two thousand names, and explained what I was looking for. His response in turn was to spend the better part of the next two weeks pestering librarians across the state of Massachusetts on my behalf, and he ended up mailing me not only photocopies of his telephone book but also links to online copies of the Boston city directory for 1963 and more information about his state's library system than I knew what to do with. I was lucky enough to have placed an ad that was seen by someone with enough time, generosity, and nimbleness of mind that he was willing to make me copies of all of this information.

I fully realize that very few readers are going to rush out to try to find an old telephone book, especially based on my recommendation. But if you will not get an old telephone book for yourself, try getting one for someone else. Find the telephone book (either yellow pages or white) from the childhood of a friend or loved one, and give it to that person the next time a present is needed.

Perhaps you'd initially be looked at askance, or worse, but I think that once anyone in this position opens the book and begins to leaf through its pages, the inherent value of such a present will become obvious. You are bequeathing not simply a book, not simply an assembly of pages and ink—you are giving a gift of memories, and so each book becomes as individual and unique as the person who is reading his or her own history through it.

7

"A SHOPPING MALL IN PRINT"

The Yellow Pages and How They Got That Way

As the year 2009 drew to a close, a number of newspapers published articles in their financial sections breathlessly trumpeting the resurgent success of an industry that had recently been thought to have fallen on hard times. Many had been predicting the incipient demise of this particular industry, as the Internet was thought to have taken large chunks of its profit margin. The resurgent industry in question was Hollywood, which had just had a record year, garnering more than ten billion dollars in ticket sales.

Ten billion of anything is quite a formidable number, whether it is grains of sand or units of currency. The print version of the yellow pages was taking in more than ten billion dollars per annum a decade or so ago. Within just a few years, it had grown to fourteen billion a year. The fact that so many people are willing to spend so much money on this form of advertising will likely ensure that the yellow pages will be with us for quite some time to come.

The question of what counts as the very first yellow pages is one with no clear answer, and it depends on what one thinks of as the yellow pages. Some would say that the very first telephone book, the one printed in New Haven in February 1878, was in fact the first yellow pages, or at least the direct forerunner, for the reason that it was primarily made up of business listings, which were organized by category.

Others would say that it was the one printed in Cheyenne, Wyoming, in 1881, as this was the first book that was actually printed on yellow paper. The decision to use this color paper was motivated more by necessity than by anything else—the printer had run out of white paper and just happened to have a stock of yellow paper left. It was a happy accident as, unbeknownst to the printer, future studies on the effects that various color combinations have on legibility of type would show that black type on a yellow background is the most legible color combination.[1]

A slender book titled *Events in Telephone History*, published by the AT&T information department, states that the first telephone directory featuring classified business listings on yellow paper was the one released in Detroit in April 1906 by the Michigan State Telephone Company.

Yet the R.H. Donnelley Company is of the opinion that *it* was responsible for the first yellow pages. Or, as its company history, *Donnelley and the Yellow Pages: The Birth of an Advertising Medium*, phrases it, regarding the appearance of its first classified telephone book: "the Chicago Telephone Directory of May 15, 1886, is generally acknowledged as the birth of classified telephone directory advertising."

Each of these claims is correct in some way, depending on how one defines the yellow pages. The Cheyenne directory of 1881 was indeed the very first telephone book to be printed on yellow paper. The Donnelley book printed in 1886 was the first classified directory of business listings in alphabetized sections, but it was not printed on yellow paper. And the Detroit book published by AT&T in 1906 was the first telephone book that had classified business listings printed on yellow paper. The yellow pages were not officially yellow until the early 1950s, when AT&T issued a directive that all classified business directories henceforth be printed on yellow paper only.

I would lay the blame for the first yellow pages on the shoulders of the Donnelley Company.

Some evils have been invented by individuals who were unaware of the fact, at the time of inventing, that they were causing great harm to future mankind. Benjamin Franklin, for instance, is widely regarded as being the individual who introduced the first mail-order catalog in the United States. His catalogs were a far cry from the glossy fluff that chokes our mailboxes today; Franklin's offerings, at least initially, were restricted to books of a scientific nature.

So this founding father of our country, beloved ambassador, inventor, and bon vivant, is also at least somewhat to blame for the deluge of millions and millions of pounds of junk mail, promising me cheaper garden furniture for the garden I do not have, better clothing for the job I do not want, and more general instances of superfluity than I can shake a rolled-up catalog at. Yet we do not hold the bespectacled and portly founding father responsible, for there is no evidence that he was acting with any malice toward future generations. As much as I hate catalogs, I do not blame Benjamin Franklin for their existence.

In the case of Reuben H. Donnelley, I am not so sure.

Donnelley was not only behind much of the success of the classified directory business but also one of the first businessmen to understand the potential profit that could be found in selling to business concerns the lists of subscribers to the telephone, facilitating the direct-mail industry.

The Chicago telephone directory of 1886 was the work of this Reuben H. Donnelley, who at the tender age of twenty-two had already been working in advertising and in publishing city directories for six years. Born in Ontario, Canada, in August 1864, he moved to Chicago with his family when he was two months old. His father, Richard Donnelley, was a printer himself, and he moved to the bustling midwestern city in the hopes of starting his own business.

The elder Donnelley started his own printing and publishing firm and began to print city directories for Chicago in 1873. These city directories were not the only fare he churned out—he also published a line of cheap reprints of dime novels.

The novels were short-lived, but the city directories were profitable for the Donnelley Company. There had been a city directory published in Chicago since a man named James W. Norris began printing one in 1844. Richard Donnelley's directory publishing proved to be successful enough that he opened a new branch of his business, entirely devoted to city directories, in 1880. His son, Reuben, who was still enrolled in Hyde Park High School, began working for his father the next year, learning the directory business from the bottom up. In 1886, the telephone company in Chicago awarded the Donnelleys the contract to print the Bell telephone directory. The city had had a telephone directory since 1878, the same year that most major cities began to have one. This directory included both residential telephone numbers and a classified list of business numbers within it, the latter of which had grown from a mere three pages to seventy-six in the first eight years.

This new telephone directory was the province of the twenty-one-year-old son of Richard Donnelley, who apparently had ink running through his veins, as he had shown little inclination to do anything except learn the family business. Even though he had an aptitude for selling and had cut his teeth working as a canvasser, selling advertisements door to door to the businesses listed in his family's directory, Reuben initially found that it was difficult to make any decent profits from the new telephone book.

For the first three years that he ran the telephone directory, Reuben Donnelley aggressively pursued advertisements for the book. However, in 1889 the city of Chicago passed a law forbidding advertising in the classified directory; the law lasted until 1901. This twelve-year drought notwithstanding, Donnelley was a man of vision, and he could see that the possibilities of advertising and telephone directories together could be extremely lucrative.

In the beginning of the twentieth century, Reuben Donnelley was traveling the country, actively seeking to garner contracts to print the telephone directories of large cities. He later won the contract to publish the Manhattan telephone books and then several directories in Wisconsin. Soon after, the Donnelley Company began printing the directories for other parts of New York City, including Brooklyn and Queens.

By 1915, the Chicago telephone directory had reached such a size that it was necessary to separate the business listings from the alphabetical residential ones, creating two books for the city.

The Donnelley Company was the largest printer of telephone directories for the twentieth century. By the time Reuben Donnelley passed away in 1929, he had amassed a personal fortune of over ten million dollars. By all accounts, he was a well-respected businessman, known for his honesty and civic spirit. Although a fine individual, in many ways he is responsible for the extraordinary glut of yellow pages in our midst today, for it was Reuben Donnelley, more than anyone else, who showed how lucrative selling ads in yellow pages could be.

Too Much of a Good Thing

For much of the life of the telephone, there was a monopoly (or near monopoly) on its service in the United States. AT&T (which was familiarly known as Ma Bell) operated almost all of the telephone service in the nation and, along with that, produced almost all of the telephone books. This all changed when the U.S. Department of Justice demanded the breakup of the AT&T monopoly.

In 1982, AT&T and the Justice Department finally came to an agreement as to how to divide the telephone company up—AT&T would remain in business, and there would be seven additional smaller companies, known as Regional Bell Operating Companies (better known as Baby Bells). The world's largest company would be broken into many smaller ones.

There are many aspects of the AT&T divestiture that have been written about exhaustively, and for the most part they do not have much to do with the telephone book. However, part of the divestiture ruling involved the yellow pages, granting the new telephone companies the right to publish their own, exclusively, for the next seven years. At this time, the yellow pages nationwide were taking in approximately four billion dollars a year, a not inconsiderable amount of money for the fledgling telephone companies.

For a decade or so things ran relatively smoothly. The small Bells had the right and responsibility of handling local telephone numbers. Long-distance companies that wanted to access these telephone numbers had to pay for the information. And then Congress waded in.

The Telecommunications Act of 1996 was not designed with the intent of flooding America with cheap yellow pages, but that is nonetheless what happened. The act was designed to foster competition and help lower rates among a wide variety of telecommunications firms. However, a single small clause stipulated that the local phone databases, which had previously been the sole province of the Baby Bells, now required what was referred to as nondiscriminatory access. What this translated to, more or less, was that anyone who wanted to publish a telephone directory could. And many people did.

And still do. Today, anyone who wants to can publish his or

her own copy of the yellow pages. All it takes is getting the numbers from the local telephone company and then hiring salesmen to go about selling ads.

As a result, residents in some areas in the country receive more yellow pages than they know what to do with. Some receive more than a half-dozen competing versions of the yellow pages, each of which claims to be the most authoritative guide to the commerce of the area, and each of which is making money by selling advertising space to that very commerce.

No one has taken advantage of the Telecommunications Act of 1996 by deciding to print a competing white pages. This brings up another of the obvious differences between the yellow and the white pages, aside from color and content: the yellow pages makes money, and the white pages does not. This has been apparent for quite some time; by 1951, the Chicago yellow pages already had annual revenue exceeding ten million dollars.

Selling the Yellow Pages

The yellow pages received a good deal more promotional effort on the behalf of the telephone company than the white pages ever has. Starting in 1954, it introduced the backward-named character Wolley Segap as part of a promotional drive to educate people in using the yellow pages.

The yellow pages has also had a fair share of logos and catchphrases, from the earliest one adopted by the telephone company, a depiction of an open book and the phrase "Find it fast in the Yellow Pages," to the more recent "Let your fingers do the walking," which was accompanied by the seemingly ubiquitous illustration of an open book and perambulating digits. In an extremely rare oversight for a company that zealously guarded its image, this finger-walking logo, which was created in 1961, was never trademarked, and so one of the world's most recognizable symbols fell into the public domain.

The yellow pages has also been promoted through a great deal of television and radio advertising, perhaps most notably through the stentorian tones of James Earl Jones. Choosing the man who so inimitably voiced Darth Vader—one of the most recognizable movie villains of all time—might have been considered a dubious choice, but it was a smashing success for the telephone company.

Jones appeared in a number of advertisements for Bell Atlantic throughout the 1990s, touting the company's directory assistance and yellow pages. He became so identified with the telephone company and directory assistance that when he took part in an event at the Philadelphia Free Library, people showed up carrying copies of the telephone book for him to sign.

In a somewhat lighter vein of advertising, the Yellow Pages Association of America hired comedian Jon Lovitz in the late 1990s to do a series of television ads, creating for him the persona of "the man who wrote the yellow pages." Lovitz, who had previously been a cast member of *Saturday Night Live*, was presented as the author of the classified telephone book. Some of the ads were of a decidedly oblique nature, such as the one that consisted entirely of fifteen seconds of the comedian weeping before cutting away to a shot of the yellow pages heading for the category "Tax Assistance."

Legally Bound

The yellow pages may have been advertising itself since the 1950s, but members of one of the largest commercial groups now to be found in it were not allowed to advertise themselves until late in the 1970s.

For much of the time that the telephone book has existed, both white and yellow pages, it has been illegal for lawyers to advertise their services in it. But even worse than being illegal, it was considered gauche to even want to do so. No less an authority than the chief justice of the Supreme Court, Warren Burger, told a meeting of the American Bar Association's Commission on Advertising that if he had remained in private practice, he would rather "dig ditches" than consent to advertising his services as a lawyer. One suspects that Burger either had firmly held principles or had not dug enough ditches to make an informed comparison. The chief justice also stated that clients should be advised to "never, never, never under any circumstances" retain a lawyer who commits this sin of advertising.[2]

It was not always illegal for lawyers to advertise in the pages of the telephone book. A small article in a 1905 issue of the *Central Law Journal* brings to light the promotional and unsavory activities of a barrister by the name of S. M. Thornley.

Thornley had an advertisement placed on the cover of a telephone book in Iowa, offering his services as a justice of the peace and as a notary public. Below that he stated that he was also in the business of marrying those who so desired, and he finished his ad by mentioning that he also provided divorces for those who had such a need. "Divorce court always open" read the last line—there was no mention of what the hours of instituting matrimony were.

The *Central Law Journal* took a rather dim view of such practices: "It is apparent that Mr. Thornley intends to encourage an entrance into the portals of matrimony by providing for a back door of escape. May the Lord have mercy on his soul for so foully deluding unsuspecting humanity."[3]

The Lord may have had mercy on S. M. Thornley's soul, but the American Bar Association (ABA) would likely not have. Three years after this lawyer's offending advertisement, the ABA issued its first ethics code: it allowed for its members to trumpet their services through one avenue only—printed cards.

And so as you look through the lawyers' sections in various yellow pages across America for most of the twentieth century, all you will see is row after row of neat, orderly names and telephone numbers, with nary a font over eight points in sight. There are no screaming headlines about "fighting for your rights," or fighting for anyone else's rights, for that matter. It is an oasis of typographic normalcy in the middle of a book that is punctuated with advertisements.

Several unsuccessful attempts were made to convince the ABA and the courts that lawyers should be allowed to advertise their services as a First Amendment right. But it wasn't until 1977 that the Supreme Court ruled in *Bates v. State Bar of Arizona* that it should be legal for lawyers to advertise.

And so, later that year, the American Bar Association voted to allow lawyers to begin advertising their services, so long as such ads were confined to the yellow pages and ABA-approved directories. This reminds me a bit of the statement that automotive giant Henry Ford made in his book *My Life and Work*, regarding the possibility of a customer buying one of his Model Ts in a new color: "Any customer can have a car painted any color that he wants, so long as it's black."[4]

In any event, lawyers now had the freedom to advertise their services in the yellow pages, and they appear to have taken full advantage of it. These books now have page after page of large advertisements, hawking the legal services of a wide range of members of the legal profession.

When I visited with Charles Eric Gordon, who not only collects telephone books but is also a lawyer, he took particular delight in showing me the progression of the legal advertisement in the yellow pages. In the middle of the twentieth century, the telephone book had naught but names and numbers. Shortly after the court decision allowed lawyers to advertise, a few began to take out ads, but they were for the most part rather sober affairs.

Since then, the legal profession appears to have abandoned whatever sense of decorum it might once have had, for the more recent books that Gordon pulled off his shelves to use as illustrative examples were filled with innumerable full-page color ads, each one more lurid and less restrained than the next.

One such ad had a simulated photograph of a situation that might well require a lawyer—a man who was in the process of being run over by a car. But the photograph was taken from inside the car, with the putative victim sprawled across the windshield, a look of chagrin plastered on his face as he himself was plastered across the windshield of the photographer.

Another advertisement featured what appeared to be an oil truck on its side, bursting into enormous plumes of flames. From the view presented, it looked unlikely that anyone would have survived the crash. There were pages and pages of stop-motion dramatic reenactments of all manner of hideous occurrences. Old ladies falling down stairs, children who had recently eaten a large quantity of lead paint getting ready to reap the consequences, cars and drivers suffering all manner of havoc wrought upon them—it was Dante's *Inferno*, advertised. I got the feeling that the law section of the yellow pages could function as a particularly gruesome flip book, if only my fingers were large enough to flip the pages.

Food, Cars, and Doctors

Today, lawyers are the ninth most common listing in the yellow pages, according to a report issued by the Yellow Pages Association (YPA) ranking the 287 most common listings in the book nationwide for the year 2009.[5] The top rank is occupied by "Restaurants—Fast Food, Other," which accounted for approximately 1,286,300,000 references that year. The restaurant industry narrowly beat out "Physicians and Surgeons," which had 987,400,000 mentions. Rounding out this triumvirate was the category of "Automobile Repairing and Service."

According to the YPA, there are 352 million references to auto parts in the nation's yellow pages for 2009, but this is a somewhat misleading number. When you add in the numbers for "Automobile Repairing and Service" (381 million), "Auto

Dealers—New & Used" (174 million), "Tire Dealers" (114 million), and "Automobile Renting and Leasing" (51 million), it is apparent that we are a nation that cares very much about its cars.

Somehow, the fact that food, cars, and doctors occupy the greatest amount of space in our yellow pages listings makes sense. One can easily imagine some sort of causal relationship between all of these things. If the top three groups were food, doctors, and sculpture, it would come as a shock.

What else can it tell us, this list of the things that we are interested in buying? Nothing positive, I am afraid. There is very little by way of beauty in these three hundred categories—they represent a sort of *Picture of Dorian Gray* featuring the American consumer, illustrating in a cold and mercenary light exactly what things we most often choose to spend our consumer dollars on, reflected back at us by the amount of reciprocal advertising invested in the yellow pages.

Pizzerias and dentists are in the top ten, as are plumbing contractors and department stores. Immediately after the top ten there are hospitals, beauty salons, and insurance agents, suggesting that we are a people who are in a constant state of physical decrepitude or that we anticipate being so.

It is nice to see that florists occupy a higher spot on the list (#18) than banks do (#19). But it is slightly depressing to see that pet groomers are so much more commonly listed (#36) than bicycle stores (#127). And how should we interpret the fact that musical instrument stores and junkyards had the same number of listings in the 2008 yellow pages (13.2 million)?

What does it say about us that there are more listings in the yellow pages for "Golf Courses Public" than there are for "Book

Dealers Retail"? How do we interpret the fact that we have so many nursing homes that this category ranks sixtieth in the yellow pages?

And why in the world is "Carpet & Rug Cleaners" the twenty-second most populous category in the yellow pages, ahead of such other seemingly more useful and necessary elements of life as schools, bakeries, and libraries? Does this mean that we are a nation of people who own filthy carpets . . . or very clean ones? Or does it simply mean that we are a nation of people who worry greatly about the cleanliness of our carpets?

It is depressing to wade through these three hundred categories and see the unvarnished truth of what we are concerned with. It is stunningly mundane. An article in the *New York Times* in 1987 contained a quote from an advertising executive who was waxing rhapsodic about the potential of the yellow pages: "It is a shopping mall in print."[6] There may be nothing wrong with individual stores in a shopping mall, but when one looks at them en masse and sees how much unnecessary garbage they are trafficking in, one cannot help but feel a bit unwell.

8

RIPPED IN HALF

The Story Behind a Storied Tradition

Ripping a telephone book in half has been seen as a sign of strength ever since telephone books became large enough that they looked difficult to rip through.* This trick has long been a staple of professional strongmen, enough so that telephone companies used to keep an additional stock of out-of-date books around, so that they could provide them to people who wanted to destroy a telephone book.

Galen Gough was one such strongman who ripped his way through a good number of the telephone company's excess books. Gough (also known by the slightly less euphonious name of Galen Gotch) had lied his way into the marines at the age of

---

* They have also served to demonstrate a lack of strength, as when Clark Gable unsuccessfully attempted to tear one in half in George Sidney's 1950 film *Key to the City.*

sixteen, so that he might fight in World War I. He managed to successfully join and had a good portion of his head damaged by shrapnel for his troubles.

Gough's left mastoid region was pierced by a piece of high explosive (which translates, more or less, to something metal moving at high speed poking him in the brain), resulting in paralysis on the left side of his face and an inability to use his right arm or leg. For three years following this event he was unable to walk. Gough forced himself through a series of grueling exercises, which proved efficacious enough that within a span of several more years, he was widely acclaimed as the strongest man in the world.

Gough performed many strongman stunts that would be considered relatively normal, such as simply lifting heavy weights. But he also showed a proclivity for stunts that seem to be somewhat east of sane, as is evidenced by his habit of lying down and letting large automobiles (and small trucks) run over his stomach (something he did more than a thousand times),[1] or hanging off a rope on an airplane, holding on only with his teeth.

Gough also liked to rip telephone books in half and was one of the first strongmen to make use of this new medium of impressing people. Prior to ripping apart telephone books, strongmen would tear decks of playing cards in half (which sounds quite impressive by itself, but Gough would sometimes rip three or four decks in half at once).

Gough spent many years touring the country, hanging from airplanes, letting motor vehicles full of passengers run him over, and visiting death and destruction on innumerable telephone books. But he was not simply a creature of brawn; he had an artistic side, exhibited by the fact that later in his career he became a painter. His work was shown in the Arthur U. Newton Galleries in New York City, on Fifty-seventh Street, just off of Fifth Avenue,[2] and in shows in other cities. Galen Gough passed away in 1962, still in his early sixties. This was a relatively young age, but long in the tooth compared to another noted telephone book ripper, Harry Luft.

Harry Luft, known as "the Brooklyn Samson," had an unnatural strength at an early age. He also passed away at an unnaturally early age, succumbing to what his obituary obliquely referred to as an "organic disease."[3] But in his brief time on this earth, Luft demonstrated that youth is no impediment to performing tasks that are essentially useless yet strangely compelling nonetheless.

Even though he stood but five feet, four inches, and weighed less than 150 pounds, Luft was capable of towing a car with his teeth or a single finger. Subsisting on a diet that consisted entirely of vegetables, Luft attributed his superior strength and vigor to his practice of calisthenics. But although he was freakishly strong in many other ways, it was in the area of telephone book ripping that Luft demonstrated true mastery.

Other strongmen might tear apart a single volume of varying thickness—such a feat would not have impressed this seventeen-year-old Brooklynite. Harry Luft would rip two New York City telephone books in half at the same time (each one of these books was some two thousand pages). I've seen a picture of him performing this, midrip, and he looks as though he is exerting the same amount of physical effort that I might in trying to pick what shirt I want to wear.[4]

Lest you think that this trick, this feat of strength, is solely the province of the Y chromosome, there have been female telephone rippers. A 1950 article in the journal *Telephony* describes Virve Simovart as a "Brooklyn schoolgirl weighing 128 pounds" who can tear a telephone book in half "without even drawing a deep breath."

Unfortunately, there is little additional information about Simovart, and so I have no idea if she went on to further directory-ripping glories, or if she contented herself with a youthful obsession with tearing numbers. At the same time that young Virve was helping establish Brooklyn as a place that is overly representative of people who like to rip telephone books, another woman was also ripping them, and with better publicity.

Joan Rhodes, an English strongwoman and former model, was known as "the Mighty Mannequin." She performed her routine in music halls throughout Europe, lifting audience members over her head, breaking six-inch nails in half in her hands, and ripping telephone books with the best of them.[5]

In his book *Bob Hope: A Life in Comedy*, William Robert Faith describes the act that Rhodes had worked out with Hope when the two of them were touring in Iceland, performing for American troops in the 1950s: "Hope would be singing 'Embraceable You' alone onstage when Joan would walk out seductively and without warning lift Hope up into her arms and cuddle him while he was still singing."

This routine was a rousing success until a show in Keflavik, Iceland, when it was decided that Rhodes should hold Hope over her head and then spin him around. After a few spins one of them lost their balance, with the result that Hope was dropped on his head on the cement floor.[6]

Phone Book Ripping in Our Times

Although this trick has largely been the province of strongmen of yore, part and parcel with biting nails in half, lifting small cows, and tossing logs, it is still very much alive as a practice. In fact, it has even taken on an air of competition, as men (and the occasional woman) with overly strong fingers vie with one another to tear more telephone books than their peers.

In 2005, the world record for telephone book destruction by hand was set by a Californian named Ed Shelton, who ripped through fifty-five telephone books in about three minutes. Shelton held his title for little more than a year, however, as he was dethroned by the man who had held the title several times since 2002: Ed Charon, an evangelical Christian minister whose fingers were large enough that he wore a size 16½ ring (the average man's ring size is about a 10, and the largest size typically available is a 12).

Charon came to the business of ripping telephone books late in life; he didn't rip one until 1998, after he saw the stunt performed on television. Although possessed of inordinately powerful hands, possibly as the result of a youth spent working as a heavy-equipment operator, he lacked the requisite strength, or technique, to rip with abandon without training. And so Ed Charon trained himself at ripping telephone books. I suppose it is possible that there have been others who have approached this endeavor with the same amount of gusto and determination, but it seems quite unlikely, for if there had been, there would be very few telephone books left; in training himself to become a champion telephone book ripper, Charon ripped sixty-five thousand of them.

I don't suppose many of us wake up in the morning and decide that what we would like to do with our day is rip one hundred telephone books in half, but that is what Charon did, for months on end. For he saw something in telephone books that few other people see, which was a way to reach audiences that had nothing at all to do with telephoning them.

Shortly after seeing his first telephone book ripped on television, Charon realized that being able to perform this feat could offer him a potent way of communicating to the audiences that he most often preached to as a minister—the young and the criminals.

While addressing these two audiences, schoolchildren and incarcerated people, Charon would enumerate a litany of addictions and instances of sinful behavior, pausing at each one to rip in half a telephone book of increasing size. Crying "God can break those habits!" at the finale, he would split in half a one-thousand-page book.

Charon always ripped his books from top to bottom, which was the only way that he considered it "legal" to do and still claim that you had ripped the book. Any other method employed he would refer to as "the girl's way," which makes it obvious that he had never made the acquaintance of Joan Rhodes or of Tina Shelton (the wife of Ed), who herself ripped twenty-one telephone books in half in three minutes in 2005.

He first set a world record for telephone books ripped in 2002, making his way through nineteen copies of the Southwestern Bell yellow pages in three minutes, 1,100 pages each. Later that year he lost his title, when a fitness instructor from Indiana ripped thirty books. Charon regained his throne in 2004 by ripping thirty-nine copies of the Portland white pages. The telephone book of this Oregonian city was always Charon's favorite one to rip, as it had the thinnest pages.

After Ed Shelton took the title in 2005 with his seemingly impregnable record of fifty-five books ripped in three minutes, the *New York Times* saw fit to place this feat in the special pantheon of "records that are not likely to be broken anytime soon," alongside Joe DiMaggio's fifty-six-game hitting streak of 1941 and Lance Armstrong's seven consecutive Tour de France victories. This was apparently enough to rouse Ed Charon, who at the age of seventy ripped fifty-six Portland white pages in the requisite time to once more reclaim his crown. Charon died shortly thereafter, at the age of seventy-one, of a heart attack.[7]

The art of tearing telephone books in half is perhaps not the most serious form of competition known to man. But before we pass judgment on Ed Shelton, Ed Charon, or any other aficionado of this sport, we should acknowledge that it is far from the most frivolous activity that people engage in; I will invoke here the worldwide cellular-telephone-throwing championships, hosted by Finland since the year 2000. Or perhaps you've seen curling in the Winter Olympics. Enough said.

Every year, Finland hosts the world's cellular-telephone-throwing championships. This is exactly what it sounds like—an event to see who can throw a cellular phone the greatest distance. The festival organizers describe it as a "light and modern Finnish sport" and claim that it is "the only sport where you can pay back all the frustrations and disappointments caused by these modern equipments."[8]

Competitors cannot just throw any phone they feel like; there are regulations that must be followed. Each thrown phone must weigh at least 220 grams. There are two categories, one for pure distance and another that is more concerned with the style and élan demonstrated by the tossers. The current world record holder for the cell phone thrown the greatest distance belongs to Mikko Lampi, who in 2005 managed to throw his telephone 311 feet, 7 inches.

Trade Secrets

At this point, some of you might be wondering if you yourself might be able to rip a telephone book in half. (Some of you might also be wondering how far you could throw your cellular phone, but I can't help you there.) Perhaps you are casting a covetous glance over at the chunky volume residing next to your home telephone (if you indeed still have either a land line or the chunky book that used to reside next to it). Rest assured, should you care to rip a telephone book life from limb, you *can* learn to do so. Although many of the strongmen (and women) who have performed this feat have done so unaided by chicanery, there are some shortcuts to help you accomplish this seemingly enormous feat of strength.

The easiest way to cheat, provided you have the time to do so, is the "soak and bake" method. Any telephone book that is completely immersed in water and then baked in an oven until dry (use extreme caution, and please remember that 451 degrees Fahrenheit is more than just a book title—any hotter than this and your book will ignite)* will change its composition. It will become brittle enough that with relatively little effort it can be almost snapped in half. It may be apocryphal, but I have heard that this was the method of preparing the telephone book that Lindsay Wagner, playing the Bionic Woman, ripped asunder in the television show of the late 1970s. It is of note that this scene, in which the Bionic Woman terrifies a group of unruly schoolchildren who are unlucky enough to have drawn her as a substitute teacher, was deemed representative enough of her physical prowess that it was chosen as one of the few images worthy to grace the side of a lunchbox designed as a tie-in to this television show.

Another method of ripping the phone book is based on the principle that as long as you fan the pages out before you begin ripping, it will be fairly easy to do. This way you are only ripping a small number of pages at a time rather than attempting to rip the entire book at once.

If you search on the Internet, you can find a hundred and one more ways of accomplishing this, with varying degrees, one presumes, of efficacy. You can even buy a DVD that has been produced by a genuine strongman, which purports to reveal his secrets for the best possible way to rip your telephone books.

Whatever method you choose, do not pick the one that was chosen by Steve Sparks.

* It is recommended that you not allow the temperature to exceed 200 degrees F with this method.

In 1994, Sparks was a promising young pitcher who played for a minor league team in the Milwaukee Brewers organization. He was at this time on the cusp of moving from the minor leagues to the majors, with all the attendant fame and money that is entailed in such a switch, when he happened to view a traveling group of motivational speakers (never a good idea). These speakers demonstrated the power of motivation through bending iron bars and ripping telephone books. Sparks was sufficiently impressed by this display that he attempted to replicate the feat himself and dislocated both his shoulder and his chance of making it into the major leagues that year. (Although the injury Sparks sustained certainly ranks as among the most ignominious of all sports injuries, it did not prevent him from eventually joining the major leagues and enjoying a long and fruitful career.)

I've been thinking about ripping a telephone book of my own for much of the past year. I've read about telephone book rippers of yore, and I've watched this feat a number of times on Internet videos, with varying degrees of amusement. And yet I cannot quite bring myself to do it.

Every so often I'll pick up one of the seemingly interchangeable volumes that are left on the doorstep of my apartment building, and I've noticed that I am usually the first (and frequently the only) person of the ten units in the building to take advantage of these offerings. They are always yellow pages, as this variety of phone book comes with far greater frequency. I bring it upstairs and place it somewhere near the kitchen, where it sits, unused and unripped. I've begun to anthropomorphize these books, and I wonder on occasion if they are curious and apprehensive about their fate. They are like the mice that some pet owners will bring home to feed to a snake, but which live on in a separate cage when the snake owners cannot bring themselves to sacrifice the wee beasts.

Why is it so hard to destroy a book?

The books in question are, even by the extraordinarily low standards of telephone books, in no way literary—these lower-echelon yellow pages are, at best, the airport novels of the reference world. Yet no matter how little worth they have, I cannot help but feel a wave of revulsion creeping up, gorge rising in my gullet, when I think about inflicting harm upon them.

When I happen across books that have been thrown away, I always feel a touch of despair that these volumes are so unloved that no one wants them, a feeling that extends itself even to the pallets of shrink-wrapped telephone books that I constantly see put out with crumpled newspapers, empty milk containers, and sundry recyclables. Although they are not typical books, they have enough of a bookish appearance that it is impossible for me not to extend some of the same concern that I have for volumes of greater content.

For years I would take books from the garbage when I came across them, ripping open with abandon any plastic bags or cardboard boxes I found them in on the street, or happily diving into a Dumpster filled with construction debris and a handful of wayward volumes. On rare occasions I have made spectacularly interesting finds, such as the time I happened across an enormous book from 1928, bound in red leather, titled *Automobile Safety for Twenty Million Drivers*. It was one of the earliest driving manuals ever published, and it is filled with gorgeous black-and-white photographs of New York City in the 1920s.

But far more often I would end up bringing home armfuls of biblio-orphans, books that I knew I would likely never read, in the hopes that one day I would find someone who would want to read them. Some years ago I discovered that I had thousands of these unread books and decided I needed to cull my holdings.

I tried to sell them to various used bookstores, but these purveyors of mustiness have a finely tuned sense of what will inevitably languish on their shelves, and so most of what I offered was met with demurrals of varying degrees of politeness. I ended up throwing away hundreds of books, but I carefully placed them all in conveniently open boxes near some trash cans, so that others who shared my sentiment for rescuing books from the trash might mull them over.

I am not one of those people who takes excessive care with my books. I bend the corners of pages to mark my place, I leave them lying facedown and opened up, and I will even occasionally write marginalia with pen or pencil. I do not wrap them in protective coverings. I have even heard of some people who don cotton gloves to read certain books (some libraries require this when perusing rare materials), although I have not yet met such a creature. Winston Churchill's wife was reported to wear gloves when reading the newspaper, but I believe that this was so she would not get ink smudged on her fingers.[9]

When I spoke with Gwillim Law, I asked if he had ever ripped one of his telephone books. He allowed that he had in fact ripped a single copy of the thousands that he had accumulated, and he hastened to add that it was a duplicate of one that he already owned. He said that he did it just to see what the feeling would be. I asked him what that feeling was, and he replied, "Well . . . it did feel a bit naughty."

Perhaps the naughtiest telephone book ripper in history was James Baker, a purported serial killer in the 1920s who had ripped a telephone book in half and left it scattered over the body of a man he had just killed. For a short while Baker was a media sensation, in small part due to his calling card, the ripping and scattering of a telephone book, and in larger part because he confessed to a great number of murders (reportedly eight to ten).

Newspapers reported that the police officers who were leading the interrogation teased Baker, saying that they did not think him strong enough to rip a telephone book in half, to which he responded by asking for a book to be brought to his cell. He then promptly ripped it in half in the exact same fashion as the one that had been left behind at the murder. Of course, it should be mentioned that all of this occurred during the mayoralty of Jimmy Walker (often called Beau James), under whose aegis the police department of New York reached infamously elevated levels of corruption, and so it would be advisable to take any of these reports with a few grains of salt.

There is something both ineluctably noble and sad about instances of biblio-destruction. These are all cases in which a book, or group of books, has been targeted because of some overwhelming emotion or fear. Books are burned, in almost all cases, because people truly hate the book (or what the book represents). The death of these books is also frequently a corollary to other wanton acts of destruction or violence—as in the case of the Library of Alexandria or the burning of books in Nazi Germany. In very few cases has a book been burned or otherwise destroyed simply because it was bad or because the burners felt that it had poor plot development.

There are, of course, occasional exceptions. In May 2007, the owners of a small used bookstore in Kansas City, Missouri, publicly burned a few dozen books as a means of drawing the public's attention to the fact that reading in America is in a state of decline. The owners of the store, Tom Wayne and W. E. Leathem, were not incinerating rare, leather-bound first editions, so this can presumably be taken as a sign of their displeasure with the worth of the reading material.

But for all the various ways that these books have been destroyed, and likely will continue to be destroyed in the future, they are not treated with the same callous disregard as telephone books, which are simply thrown away without much possibility of arousing any ire.

As an unregenerate lover of and collector of books, I cannot help but feel a small twinge of despair whenever I see a telephone book in the garbage. The increasing frequency of these occurrences over the recent years has not diminished the despair I feel. Perhaps the only positive aspect to seeing these books thrown away so unceremoniously is that I am rather incongruously reminded of the speech Shylock utters in the third act of *The Merchant of Venice*. I find myself thinking: Does any book deserve this fate? After all, doesn't this book have pages, text, binding, covers, and all the other things that have gone into creating great works of literature?

Admittedly, the comparison between a telephone book in the garbage and Shylock's brilliant oration on the historical mistreatment of an entire people is a bit absurd. But is it wrong to feel a pang at seeing these books moldering away in the trash? After all, it was not so very long ago that books of any variety were so valuable that they were kept locked up. In his history of how man has stored his volumes through the ages, *The Book on the Bookshelf*, Henry Petroski writes of how for a considerable length of time no one thought to create bookshelves as we know them today, for the simple reason that almost no one had enough books to make stacking them on their sides necessary.

I am not entirely in favor of abstaining from throwing books away. Indeed, there are many books that I feel deserve nothing more than a quick trip to the trash heap and should very likely have never been published in the first place. Astonishing numbers of new titles are published every year—the figure is estimated at over 250,000 in the United States alone.[10] Surely some of these titles should never have seen the light of day. And yet it still tugs at my heartstrings to see so many telephone books thrown away, often still encased in their cheap plastic wrap, obviously not just unwanted but not even judged worthy of perusal.

9

THE FUTURE OF THE PHONE BOOK

There are some people for whom the telephone book evokes naught save teeth-gnashing fury. There is for them no romance or sense of history in this book of names, addresses, and numbers. When confronted with a plastic-wrapped packet of directories placed on a doorstep or driveway, they see little except for evidence of deforestation and humanity's pitiable inability to take advantage of the glorious possibilities offered by the digital age.

These people join groups such as Ban the Phone Book, which has a website and also exists as a group on Facebook. It has a logo as well—it is similar to the old yellow pages advertisement of "Let your fingers do the walking," except that instead of fingers walking there is a depiction of a disapproving, downward-turned thumb over a green telephone book. As of this writing, this Facebook group has about 6,500 members. This seems fairly small, especially when one considers that AT&T has 182,000 fans on Facebook and Verizon has about 828,000. But what the members of Ban the Phone Book lack in numbers they make up for in vehemence.

In the comments posted on the group's Facebook page, there are people who think that the telephone book is still published in order to "keep the Phone Book Delivery Driver's Union intact." There are people who swear six ways to Sunday that they have not used a telephone book in at least twenty years. And there are people who are many sorts of aghast that we have for so long continued the practice of butchering trees to make this largely unread book.

The Facebook page offers a way to sign a petition to create an opt-in delivery program. It has a small list of statistics, some of which may in fact be accurate, stating that five million trees are killed every year to make the white pages and that taxpayers then spend seventeen million dollars to have these books recycled. This may be negative attention, but it is more consideration than the humble telephone book usually gets. There is also a page that has a number of discussions about the telephone book.

One of these discussions is titled "Most creative use of white pages?" Even here, in a forum that exists primarily to rail against the existence of the telephone book, there are signs that it can be somehow more interesting than one might imagine.

One artist writes in and tells about how she has made prosthetic body parts out of torn-out pages from the telephone book. In addition to this slightly macabre use, she points out that art students frequently use the pages for cleaning paint, and printmakers do the same for their rollers.

A woman named Jolis Paons created an entire dress out of

nothing more than part of a copy of the white pages (India-napolis, I believe). From a slight distance it looks like a delicate fabric, light gray folded hundreds of times with crisp lines that make it look like a new and special material. On closer inspec-tion, the numbers begin to become apparent, but it still doesn't look anything like a mass of crumpled and folded paper, which is essentially what it is. It instead appears to be a well-turned piece of haute couture, which I suppose it is as well.

A sixty-year-old woman writes in to remind everyone that there are people of a certain age (such as her husband, who is older than she) who never learned to use computers, and likely never will, for whom the telephone book is indispensable. She rather tartly ends her post by saying, "The most creative use of the phone book is to use it as it is meant to be used."

Perhaps not surprisingly, the founders of Ban the Phone Book are the same people who run the largest independent online telephone directory, WhitePages.com. They seem to be sane and levelheaded types, with no purpose more anarchistic in mind than to allow people to opt in if they would like to receive a tele-phone book. If one does not sign an opt-in request, then one will not receive a physical paper copy of a telephone book.

I've used the WhitePages.com site to look up telephone num-bers and people, and it is certainly far easier and more efficient than using the printed telephone book. This site also serves as a reverse directory, so that if you enter a telephone number with no name, it will helpfully supply that information. In fact, it often offers to tell me far more than I am interested in knowing.

When I looked up my parents, to see what telephonic information was available for them, WhitePages.com gave me not only their telephone number but also their address, ZIP code, and approximate ages; showed me a map that detailed where they lived; and told me exactly who else lived in their household. I suppose all of that information is readily accessible elsewhere, and it should not surprise me to find it available on the Internet. But I still found it much more than I needed to know, and that was even before I had a chance to look at the sponsored links, which offered to get me the criminal background reports on my parents and to find more than fifty singles in their area. I'm going to go out on a limb and label this as too much information.

Ban the Phone Book is by no means the only organization dedicated to hastening the demise of the telephone book. There are other groups, found in unsurprising locations such as San Francisco, that have similar aims. Phone Book Free SF states that its objective is to "reduce the negative environmental and social impacts of phone book distribution by ending the delivery of unsolicited phone books."

To this end, it is supporting legislation that was introduced in 2009 by Leland Yee, a California state senator, calling for that state to adopt an opt-in program, so that the only people who will receive a telephone book will be those who specifically ask for one.

The legislation Yee introduced is aimed at repealing a decision made by the California Public Utilities Commission in 1995, which made it a requirement that the telephone companies deliver a copy of the white pages to every one of their customers. The commission reasoned that this mandatory delivery of telephone books would cut down on the number of people who used directory assistance, although it is not clear why that itself was such a burden to the state of California.

Phone Book Free SF has no commercial ties to a directory company, as Ban the Phone Book does, and most of its efforts appear to be aimed at practical solutions. The organizers ask visitors to write to them if they have seen a large package of unused telephone books, so that someone may come by to pick them up. They throw "bring your own phone book" (BYOPB) parties, inviting attendees to show up with a copy of the phone book, which they will then recycle, with the goal of collecting twenty thousand of them. They have phone book drop boxes set up to facilitate recycling.

Even though the name of groups such as Ban the Phone Book and Phone Book Free SF would seem to indicate that they make no distinction between yellow and white, they have obviously focused their efforts on the white pages. The position of Ban the Phone Book is laid out on its home page on Facebook, which states, "White pages phone books are wasteful, help stop the waste!" The group has come to the conclusion that white pages are more wasteful than yellow, and that it will be easier to get the telephone companies to stop making them than to convince them to stop making the yellow pages.

I don't know that they are correct about the white pages being more wasteful than the yellow, but they are certainly correct in that it will be easier to get the telephone companies to stop printing them. There is very little chance that the yellow pages will go away anytime soon. In fact, there is no more chance of this than there is of any other fourteen-plus-billion-dollar-a-year industry deciding to simply fold up and cease to exist. The white pages are a different story, however.

The telephone companies are not terribly excited about printing these telephone books. It costs a good deal of money to print millions and millions of books at least once or twice a year. And then after all these books have been printed, checked for mistakes, and sent out, the telephone companies receive complaints from thousands of people who don't understand why the books still exist.

Why do the white pages still exist? When you get past all the sound and the fury involved in the postings on these anti–telephone book websites, this is a legitimate question. At the very least it seems fair to ask why we still have so many of them. It is easy to understand, albeit in a depressing fashion, why the yellow pages continue to exist—they are far too lucrative for the companies that make them to voluntarily cease doing so. But do we really still need their purely informational and untinted companion? With an ever-increasing percentage of the population relying on cellular telephones (for which there is no telephone directory), does it make sense to continue to send these unwieldy books into people's homes (or to leave them in their doorways)? It is not obvious that the telephone companies are the ones pushing for their continued existence.

AT&T has been on the forefront of many of the cutting-edge developments in telephony over the past hundred-odd years, so it seems logical that it would also be a leader in developing a way to do without the directory. It is also the nation's largest supplier of directories, sending out about 40 percent of the total number. AT&T has made attempts to at least cut back on the number of the books that it makes and sends out to customers, with some mixed results.

In February 2009, AT&T asked for and received permission from the Public Utilities Commission of Ohio to stop delivering a copy of the white pages to every telephone subscriber in the state. The commission stated that Ohio subscribers who wanted a copy of the white pages would have to call the telephone company in order to receive one. Several months later, the *Cleveland Plain Dealer* printed a notice about this new policy, along with the requisite telephone number to call if one wished to receive a copy of the white pages from the telephone company.

So many people called the number, asking to be sent white pages, that the AT&T call center was overloaded. Some people spent over an hour waiting on hold, and others were transferred to call centers in other locations, where the operators had no clue why there were irate and worried customers looking for telephone books.

Currently legislation is pending in a number of states that would require the telephone companies to change the manner in which they send out their directories. Some forms of the legislation call for an opt-in program, in which only those people who actively request a telephone book would receive one. More common is opt-out legislation, which only requires that the telephone companies not send telephone books to people who ask not to receive them.

There is a large difference between how each of these two kinds of legislation would affect the number of telephone books being sent out. Given the innate laziness of humanity, it will bring about much less change if opt-out programs are adopted and people actually have to perform an action, such as calling the telephone company, to ask that they not be sent a book.

It may be hard to believe that something so small would prove to be enough to prevent people from acting to stop the telephone books from coming to their homes, but it would appear to be borne out by places where the opt-out system is already in place.

In Norway, a country substantially more environmentally conscious than our own, the telephone company has had an opt-out policy in place for several years. The number of customers who request not to receive a copy of the telephone book is slightly less than 7 percent.

It doesn't seem as though the telephone companies would be in favor of continuing to print and ship millions of copies of the white pages. The amount of advertising in these books is minimal, and it is unlikely that the revenue this brings in would cover the cost of producing the books. In some states where phone companies have been mandated to send out a copy of the white pages to every subscriber, they are allowed to attach a surcharge to the telephone bill in order to pay for the cost of the white pages. But this is not making them any substantial amount of money.

I sent an email to the public relations department at AT&T with a list of questions regarding its plans for the white pages of the future. I received a pair of immediate and somewhat puzzled responses, by both email and telephone, from a public relations person named Steve, very politely offering to help me with my queries but betraying some degree of confusion as to why I was interested.

The questions I received in return from Steve were somewhat guarded, asking me not only for clarification as to what I wanted to know but also why I wanted to know it and what I was planning to do with this information. He asked for my name, whether I had a website that he could look at, who my publisher was, and if the book I was writing was scheduled to be published or if I was still shopping it around.

It took a few telephone conversations and email exchanges before the telephone company was convinced both that I was not allied with any kind of phone-book-banning radicals and that I had no intention of starting my own, competing, telephone book service. Once this was established, the public relations people were quite prompt in responding.

I had several queries that the AT&T public relations department proved not at all interested in answering, such as how much it cost to make each copy of the white or yellow pages ("This information is proprietary"). And for many of the other questions, the answers I received were cloaked in the sort of highly polished public relations vagueness that makes responses so measured and couched in nuance that they are essentially meaningless.

However, they did emphatically state that there are no plans to do away with the white pages, at least not at the moment. They are currently testing a program (with the not very euphonious title of Residential White Pages Consumer Choice) that will give their subscribers a say as to how they will be able to access the telephone listings: as a book, via searching online, or through the use of mobile devices.

AT&T is not alone in its desire to remove from the company the responsibility of printing and delivering millions of books of residential telephone listings. In May 2010, Verizon petitioned state regulators in New York, asking that it no longer be required to send a copy of the white pages to every one of its millions of customers in the state.

The petition, sent to the New York State Public Service Commission, is full of interesting information about people's telephone book habits. It claims that, according to a recent Gallup poll, the number of households that continue to use "standalone residential white pages has dropped from 25% in 2005 to only 11% in 2008." The petition points out that Verizon is legally obligated to send telephone books to the 89 percent of households that do not use them.

As a solution Verizon offers to institute a new policy, whereby anyone who wants a telephone book (on paper or on CD) can simply ask and they'll receive one. Verizon notes in the petition that in the other states where telephone companies have been allowed to institute such a policy, "very few customers have actually requested a copy (about 2%)."[1]

It is perhaps of note that Verizon has provided information about the increasing numbers of customers who are less inclined to use the white pages, and how many tons of paper would be saved each year by not giving one to everyone (about five thousand tons), but makes no mention of whether these same customers are similarly less inclined to use the yellow pages, and how many tons of paper would be saved by not printing those books as well.

It is easy to make the assumption that the Internet will do away with the telephone book. After all, it performs all of the same functions, but it does so more efficiently and at a considerably lower cost. It would appear to be inevitable that once everyone has an Internet connection, the books themselves will be left behind.

Except that this same assumption has been made about a number of other things that the Internet was supposed to replace completely and yet which have managed to continue hobbling along in coexistence with the new technology. The old and antiquated method of sending letters, now colloquially known as "snail mail," has not disappeared, even though email is indubitably far cheaper and faster. Television sets have not disappeared, replaced in their living room ubiquity by larger and larger computer monitors.

The imminent demise of such institutions as bookstores has been trumpeted for years. While it is true that the Internet has changed the way these stores operate, they will certainly not disappear completely anytime soon.

Bill Gates has made some famous predictions about how the Internet will change the way we interact with printed material. He has stated that "reading is going to go completely online"; television will be watched on the computer, with ads targeted to each individual consumer; and the paper yellow pages will soon not be used by anyone under the age of fifty.[2]

When one of the richest men in the world makes such pronouncements, it is tempting to point out that he also made the
claim in 2004 that "two years from now spam will be solved."[3]

There is no question that telephone books are a tremendous waste
of paper, although the people who make these books and the
people who protest them disagree greatly as to how many trees
are being slaughtered for the production of the books. Many of
the companies that produce the telephone books disagree with
the assertion that their industry kills five million trees every
year, pointing out that the vast majority of these books are made
from recycled paper and sawdust salvaged from paper mills.

There is also not a doubt that many of the people who receive
them find them to be, at best, a minor nuisance. I cannot fault
the environmental goals of those who are working to see that
fewer of these unread books are sent out. Yet I also cannot help
but wonder at the level of umbrage that they bring out. Are
telephone books more deserving of extinction than other wasteful uses of paper? Why are there not more people protesting
newspapers?

My suspicion is that the reason people are targeting the white
pages is that not only are they largely unnecessary, but we've
already seen it demonstrated that we can get along without them.
There is no telephone directory for cellular phones, and that has
not prevented these devices from functioning.

According to a survey published semiannually by the Cellular Telephone Industries Association, there were approximately
2,691,793 cellular phone subscribers in the United States in 1989.

Twenty years later, that number has leaped to 276,610,580, an increase of more than a hundredfold.

This means that somewhere in the neighborhood of 90 percent of the people in the United States have a cellular telephone. And yet none of them have a copy of the white pages to rely on. Over the past few decades, as cellular phones grew from a niche luxury item to a seemingly indispensable part of modern life, there have been a number of attempts to create a directory of names and telephone numbers. For a variety of reasons, this endeavor has so far failed.

There is no cellular monopoly in the United States, and it has proved difficult to get all the disparate companies to agree to share their information. In 2004, almost all of them had agreed to set up a cellular directory, but Verizon, which with forty million customers was the largest carrier at the time, refused to join in.

In addition to the difficulties presented by getting rival companies to share their telephone numbers, there is a deep-rooted suspicion among Americans that they will be barraged by telemarketers if they make their cellular numbers available. The fact that it is already illegal for telemarketers to call people on their cellular phones has done nothing to convince people that they would rather not be listed where the telemarketers can find them.

It would be difficult to make the case that not having a white pages for the cellular phone industry has hampered its growth substantially, given how successful it has been. And given that most of the people who provide directory assistance at the telephone companies stopped using paper directories in the 1970s (they first switched to microfilm and then to computers), it is also difficult to make the case that it is imperative that the telephone companies continue to make them.

Whenever there is a discussion, or a debate, about why it is that telephone companies continue to print the white pages, there is invariably mention of the fact that some small portion of the population does not have access to the Internet or that some people who have used the telephone book all their lives just don't understand how to make the transition from newsprint to hyperlink.

But there will always be some portion of the population that does not keep up with the current technology, whether it is because they are Luddites by choice or because technology has simply passed them by. This in itself is not enough of a reason to insist on continuing to print the white pages.

It should be enough that some people just prefer to have the feel of paper on their hands when they are reading something. I know I do.

FINAL NOTE

If, after reading some of the story of this book of millions of stories, you still doubt whether it has the power to evoke feelings and memories, and to move a reader, find yourself an old paper copy and spend some time traipsing through the narrative of these names, both familial and given.

See for yourself if this humble compendium of crudely printed telephone numbers and awkwardly worded advertisements cannot elicit the sensations, feelings, and even the smells of a time in life long since past.

If, as you glance down these neatly ordered paths of vestigial memories, you are not moved to sit down and revisit this past, then you are perhaps not the kind of person that is moved by any other book, and the telephone book holds no more or no fewer glories for you than would any other work of literature.

But if you can bring yourself to invest some portion of your imagination in these names and numbers, in this text that is unencumbered by plot, then you will find something there to tickle the part of your brain that loves to read a story, whether it be romance, adventure, tragedy, or farce. And when you have discovered a story hidden in this book, think of how much easier it will be to embrace the stories in the books whose authors have actually tried to write one.

But in the meantime, glance through the telephone book every once in a while, and pay some small amount of attention to the book that is so often ignored by so many. Don't bother to read it from beginning to end; dip in and take an exploratory sip.

Read over the hundreds of listings of Brown, Schwartz, or Rodriguez, or whatever names happen to be most prevalent in the book held in your lap. Compose your own story based on the characters you meet there, even as you know almost nothing of them.

This is a volume of wishes, lies, and dreams, each and every page containing the makings of a story untrammeled by anything except your willingness to invest in it.

This is a work that is steeped in the history of the humanity within it, and your experience in browsing through it is fettered only by your imagination.

This is a book that is as boring and quotidian, or as vibrant and alive, as you choose to make it.

FURTHER READING

Although there has been very little written on the telephone book, there has been a great amount written on the subject of the telephone. For the true telephone enthusiast, Herbert Casson's *History of the Telephone* is an early and influential history. It also has the benefit of having passed into the public domain and thus may be found for free on the Internet. Similarly, *The Telephone and Telephone Exchanges*, written by John E. Kingsbury in 1915, can be downloaded online, and has much useful (and much useless) information.

For those who are interested in the social history of the telephone, Claude Fischer's *America Calling: A Social History of the Telephone to 1940* is a fine book to dig in with. And for the pro–Elisha Gray faction, and those who are interested in conspiracy theories of all stripes, *The Telephone Gambit: Chasing Alexander Graham Bell's Secret* by Seth Shulman presents a very convincing argument that we have awarded the mantle of telephone inventor to the wrong man.

You could also go to your local library and ask to see some old telephone books. The more that people ask for telephone books, the greater their chances for survival in our increasingly pressed-for-space libraries.

NOTES

INTRODUCTION

1 "Old Red Books Never 'Die,' the Ink Just Fades Away," *Chicago Tribune*, December 26, 1963, p. D5.

2 Elinor Siegel, "It's a Phone Book, Too," *New York Times Magazine*, February 10, 1946, p. 102.

3 "Phone Books as Armor," *New York Times*, July 9, 1949, p. 28.

4 *Telephone News*, June 1936, p. 4.

1. THE FIRST PHONE BOOK

1 George P. Oslin, *The Story of Telecommunications* (Macon, GA: Mercer University Press, 1999), p. 217.

2 Robert V. Bruce, "Gray, Elisha," American National Biography Online, February 2000.

3 Herbert Casson, *The History of the Telephone* (Chicago: A. C. McClurg, 1910).

4 *The Musical Times and Singing-Class Circular* (London: Novello, March 1, 1900), p. 170.

5 Freeman G. Henry, *Language, Culture, and Hegemony in Modern France* (Birmingham, AL: Summa Publishing, 2008), p. 169.

6   *The Musical Times and Singing-Class Circular* (London: Novello, March 1, 1900), p. 171.

7   Steve Mirsky, "Perfect Pitch Related to Language," *Scientific American*, May 21, 2009, www.scientificamerican.com/podcast/episode.cfm?id=63085FD0 -B68E-E5AE-81101B02FE900162 (accessed January 9, 2010).

8   John Timbs, ed., *The Year-Book of Facts in Science and Art* (London: Simpkin, Marshall, and Co., 1845).

9   "From a Correspondent," *Times* (London), September 22, 1880, p. 7.

10 *Yale News*, February 21, 1878, http://digital.library.yale.edu/cdm/document .php?CISOROOT=/yale-ydn&CISOPTR=16519&REC=21 (accessed January 9, 2010).

11 *American Telephone Journal*, July 1925, p. 29.

12 "The Early Years: George Willard Coy," *Southern New England Telephone Company: The First Fifty Years, 1878–1928*, University of Connecticut, University Libraries: Thomas J. Dodd Research Center, http://doddcenter.uconn .edu/exhibits/snet/firstfifty/earlyhistory/coy.htm (accessed May 20, 2010).

13 "The Early Years: New Haven District Telephone Company," *Southern New England Telephone Company: The First Fifty Years, 1878–1928*, University of Connecticut, University Libraries: Thomas J. Dodd Research Center, http:// doddcenter.uconn.edu/exhibits/snet/firstfifty/earlyhistory/index.htm (accessed May 20, 2010).

14 Ibid.

15 "Site of the First Telephone Exchange," National Historic Landmarks Program, www.nps.gov/nhl/DOE_dedesignations/Telephone.htm (accessed May 20, 2010).

16 Dennis Overbye, "Among Scientific Treasures, a Gem," *New York Times*, June 10, 2008, www.nytimes.com/2008/06/10/science/10auct.html (accessed May 24, 2010).

17 "The Operators," *Southern New England Telephone Company: The First Fifty Years, 1878–1928*, University of Connecticut, University Libraries: Thomas J. Dodd Research Center, http://doddcenter.uconn.edu/exhibits/snet/firstfifty/ operators/notice.htm (accessed May 20, 2010).

18 "A Doctor Expelled," *New York Times*, April 17, 1883, p. 5.

19 "Dr. E. L. Thomson Dies; Oldest Telephone User," *New York Times*, June 22, 1934, p. 21.

2. "IT TALKS!"

1 Stephen Vail, "Early Days of the First Telegraph Line," *The Making of America (Labor)*, ed. Robert Marion La Follette (Chicago: The Making of America Co., 1906), p. 474.

2 *Events in Telephone History* (New York: American Telephone and Telegraph Co., 1964), p. 27.

3 "Exhibition Facts," Free Library of Philadelphia, http://libwww.library.phila.gov/CenCol/exhibitionfax.htm (accessed May 20, 2010).

4 "Corliss, George Henry," Encyclopædia Britannica Online, www.britannica.com/EBchecked/topic/1515841/George-Henry-Corliss (accessed May 24, 2010).

5 "The 1876 Centennial Exposition," *Dial-Log*, ed. Jody Georgeson, The Telecommunications History Group Inc., Summer 2009, www.telcomhistory.org/NewsletterArchivesSummer2009.shtml#1876 (accessed May 20, 2010).

6 Lewis Mumford, *The Brown Decades: A Study of the Arts in America, 1865–1895* (Toronto: General Publishing, 1971), p. 16.

7 Russell Lynes, *The Taste-Makers* (New York: Hamish Hamilton, 1954), p. 115.

8 "A South American Lincoln," *Southwestern Telephone News*, March 1926, p. 8.

9 Ibid.

10 Francis Jehl, *Menlo Park Reminiscences*, vol. 1 (Dearborn, MI: Edison Institute, 1936), p. 101.

11 Herbert Casson, *The History of the Telephone* (Chicago: A. C. McClurg, 1911), p. 43.

12 Ibid., p. 44.

13 "Report of the Select Committee on Land Titles and Transfer," House of Commons, 1879.

14 *Telephone Magazine*, June 1934, p. 2.

15 "The Future of the Telephone," *Dial-Log*, ed. Jody Georgeson, The Telecommunications History Group Inc., Winter 2008, www.telcomhistory.org/NewsletterArchivesWinter2008.shtml (accessed May 19, 2010).

16 "Telephone Fiends," *American Telephone Journal*, September 19, 1901, p. 177.

17 "Letter to SNET, July 1888," *Southern New England Telephone Company: The First Fifty Years, 1878–1928*, University of Connecticut, University Libraries: Thomas J. Dodd Research Center, http://doddcenter.uconn.edu/exhibits/snet/firstfifty/earlyhistory/1888letter.htm (accessed May 20, 2010).

18 "Rates for Domestic Letters, 1863–2009," U.S. Postal Service, May 2009, www.usps.com/postalhistory/_pdf/DomesticLetterRates1863-2009.pdf (accessed May 20, 2010).

19 "Steamboats," U.S. Postal Service, September 2003, www.usps.com/postalhistory/_pdf/Steamboats.pdf (accessed May 20, 2010).

20 "Literacy from 1870 to 1979," National Center for Education Statistics, http://nces.ed.gov/naal/lit_history.asp (accessed May 20, 2010).

21 "The Pony Express," U.S. Postal Service, August 2008, www.usps.com/postalhistory/_pdf/PonyExpress.pdf (accessed May 20, 2010).

22 "Airmail," U.S. Postal Service, August 2008, www.usps.com/postalhistory/_pdf/Airmail.pdf (accessed May 20, 2010).

23 "Missile Mail," U.S. Postal Service, July 2008, www.usps.com/postalhistory/_pdf/MissileMail.pdf (accessed May 19, 2010).

24 Tomas Nonnenmacher, "History of the U.S. Telegraph Industry," EH.net Encyclopedia, ed. Robert Whaples, August 14, 2001, http://eh.net/encyclopedia/article/nonnenmacher.industry.telegraphic.us (accessed May 20, 2010).

25 Pamela M. Henson, "Dyar, Harrison Gray, Jr.," American National Biography Online, February 2000.

26 George P. Oslin, *The Story of Telecommunications* (Macon, GA: Mercer University Press, 1999), p. 21.

27 "Alfred Vail Was Morse's Partner; He Helped Make the Telegraph a Success—Light on Early Days," *New York Times*, May 8, 1894, p. 5.

28 Dorothea N. Spear, *Bibliography of American Directories Through 1860* (Worchester, MA: American Antiquarian Society, 1961).

29 Charles P. Kimball, *The San Francisco City Directory* (San Francisco: Journal of Commerce Press, 1850).

30 Raymond Hernandez, "Manhattan, Short on (212)'s, Will Get a Second Area Code," *New York Times*, November 25, 1997, p. A1.

31 "Customs: Give Me Liberty," *Time*, July 13, 1962.

32 *Popular Science Monthly*, vol. 88 (New York: Modern Publishing, January–June 1916), "Putting Speed in Telephone Directories," no. 5 (May 1916), p. 718.

33 Ibid.

34 Katharine and Henry F. Pringle, "Sixty Million Headaches Every Year," *Saturday Evening Post*, April 3, 1954, p. 27.

3. OF CUTTLEFISH AND POETRY

1 James J. Rawls and Richard J. Orsi, eds., *A Golden State: Mining and Economic Development in Gold Rush California* (Berkeley: University of California Press, 1999), p. 9.

2   "Language Use and English-Speaking Ability: 2000," *Census 2000 Brief*, U.S. Census Bureau, October 2003, www.census.gov/prod/2003pubs/c2kbr-29.pdf (accessed May 24, 2010).

3   *San Francisco Chronicle*, September 17, 1978, p. 7.

4   Barry Popik, "Spirit of Communication (Golden Boy)," October 17, 2004, www .barrypopik.com/index.php/new_york_city/entry/spirit_of_communication _golden_boy (accessed May 20, 2010).

5   *Hartford Courant*, December 24, 1968, p. 13B.

4. LIVING BY THE BOOK

1   Stanley Edgar Hyman, "Comment," *New Yorker*, April 1, 1944, p. 19.

2   John Faber, *Great News Photos and the Stories Behind Them* (Mineola, NY: Dover Publications, 1978).

3   Daniel Tammet, *Born on a Blue Day* (New York: Free Press, 2007).

4   Douglas R. Hofstadter, *Metamagical Themas: Questing for the Essence of Mind and Pattern* (New York: Basic Books, 1985), p. 125.

5   Tom Cheche, *Exit 10: A Sporting Life Just Off the Jersey Turnpike* (Minneapolis: Mill City Press, 2009).

6   "Memory Feats and Memory World Records," Memorable Carvello, www .memorablecarvello.co.uk/memoryworldrecords.htm (accessed May 20, 2010).

5. THE PHONE BOOK HALL OF FAME

1   Gwillim Law, "Collecting Telephone Books," Old Telephone Books, www .oldtelephonebooks.com/pbcoll.html (accessed May 20, 2010).

2   Ronald Bergan, *The Life and Times of the Marx Brothers* (New York: Smithmark, 1992), p. 91.

6. READING THE PHONE BOOK

1   Julia Vitullo-Martin and J. Robert Moskin, *Executive's Book of Quotations* (New York: Oxford University Press, 1994).

2   Elmore Leonard, "Writers on Writing: Easy on the Adverbs, Exclamation Points and Especially Hooptedoodle," *New York Times*, June 16, 2001.

3   Jay Walz, "Carolinian Sets Talking Record; Thurmond Outdoes Morse's 22 Hours 26 Minutes in '53—Latter Stayed on Feet Second Mark Passed," *New York Times*, August 30, 1957.

4   Elizabeth Landau, "A Filibuster at Princeton, to Send Frist a Message," *New York Times*, May 6, 2005.

5   Alex Mindin, "It's the Scent That Tickles the Memory," *New York Times*, November 15, 2009.

6   "Campaigns: Fire Meets Desire," Burger King Brands Inc., 2009, www .bk.com/en/us/campaigns/fire-meets-desire.html (accessed January 9, 2010).

7   John Ogden Whedon and E. B. White, "Comment," *New Yorker*, April 10, 1937, p. 13.

8   Lillian Ross, Jane Boutwell, Wallace White, S. Black, and Brendan Gill, "The Talk of the Town: Tally," *New Yorker*, August 15, 1964, p. 23.

9   Susan Sheehan, "The Talk of the Town: Agnews," *New Yorker*, August 1, 1970, p. 19.

7. "A SHOPPING MALL IN PRINT"

1   Faber Birren, *Functional Color* (New York: Crimson Press, 1937), p. 48.

2   Stephen Chapman, "The Chief Justice Throws a Tantrum," *Chicago Tribune*, July 12, 1985.

3   *Central Law Journal*, ed. Alexander H. Robbins (St. Louis: Central Law Journal Company, 1905), p. 192.

4   Fred Shapiro, *The Yale Book of Quotations* (New Haven, CT: Yale University Press, 2006), p. 282.

5   "The 2005–2009 YPA Local Media Tracking Study: Top PYP Headings—Rank Order," Yellow Pages Research Institute, www.ypassociation.org/ AM/Template.cfm?Section=Research_Institute&Template=/CM/Content Display.cfm&ContentID=3334 (accessed May 24, 2010).

6   Phillip H. Dougherty, "Competition Grows in the Yellow Pages," *New York Times*, December 22, 1987.

8. RIPPED IN HALF

1   *Washington Post*, October 6, 1923.

2   "New Exhibitions Crowd Art Week," *New York Times*, November 2, 1958, p. 126.

3   *Albany Evening News*, May 27, 1929.

4   "Harry Luft, the Brooklyn Samson," Oldtime Strongman Blog, July 10, 2009, www.oldtimestrongman.com/blog/labels/Phonebook%20Tearing.html (accessed May 24, 2010).

5   Christopher Woodward, *The London Palladium: The Story of the Theatre and Its Stars* (West Yorkshire, UK: Jeremy Mills, 2009).

6   "A Look at the World's Week," *Life* 40, no. 2 (January 9, 1956), p. 36.

7   "Recycled Fun," *Dial-Log*, ed. Jody Georgeson, The Telecommunications History Group Inc., Summer 2007, www.telcomhistory.org/NewsletterArchives Summer2007.shtml#fun (accessed May 20, 2010).

8   "Mobile Phone Throwing World Championships," www.savonlinnafestivals .com/en_Stoori.pdf (accessed May 20, 2010).

9   Brian Viner, "Vanessa Redgrave: Nothing Like a Dame," *Independent*, July 10, 2002, www.independent.co.uk/news/people/profiles/vanessa-redgrave -nothing-like-a-dame-647893.html (accessed May 20, 2010).

10   "Bowker Reports U.S. Book Production Declines 3% in 2008, but 'On Demand' Publishing More Than Doubles," Publishing Central, May 19, 2009, http://publishingcentral.com/blog/book-publishing/bowker-reports -us-book-production-declines-3-in-2008-but-on-demand-publishing-more -than-doubles?si=1 (accessed May 20, 2010).

9. THE FUTURE OF THE PHONE BOOK

1   Petition of Verizon New York Inc. for Waiver of New York Code of Rules and Regulations, Title 16, § 602.10(b) Pertaining to the Distribution of Telephone Directories, May 7, 2010, http://documents.dps.state.ny.us/public/Common/ ViewDoc.aspx?DocRefId={60B5616E-361C-4DC1-9F7B-7C800B8B2AD8} (accessed May 20, 2010).

2   "Bill Gates: Microsoft Strategic Account Summit 2007," Microsoft News Center, May 8, 2007, www.microsoft.com/Presspass/exec/billg/speeches/2007/ 05-082007MSNSASBillg.mspx (accessed May 20, 2010).

3   Joel Arak, "Gates: Spam to Be Canned by 2006," CBS News, January 24, 2004, www.cbsnews.com/stories/2004/01/24/tech/main595595.shtml (accessed May 20, 2010).

INDEX

Ammon Shea has enjoyed a range of jobs of the variety traditionally held by writers: subway musician in Paris, gondolier in San Diego, and furniture mover in New York. He lives in Manhattan with his wife, dog, and child, and may frequently be found in one library or another, complaining peevishly about the lack of non-narrative texts.